THE ART OF EXISTENTIAL COUNSELING

THE ART OF
EXISTENTIAL
COUNSELING

ADRIAN VAN KAAM, PH. D.

DIMENSION BOOKS

WILKES-BARRE, PENNSYLVANIA

Published by Dimension Books, Inc.
Wilkes-Barre, Pennsylvania

Chapter Six of this volume, "Therapeutic Attitudes," is a revised and enlarged version of an article entitled "Counseling from the Viewpoint of Existential Psychology" which first appeared in *The Harvard Educational Review,* Fall, 1962. Chapter Seven, "The Goals of Counseling and Psychotherapy from the Existential Viewpoint," is scheduled to appear in *The Goals of Psychotherapy,* an anthology edited by Alvin R. Mahrer, Ph.D., which will be published by Appleton-Century-Crofts later this year.

Library of Congress Catalog Card Number 66-27468
Copyright © 1966 by Adrian van Kaam

THE ART OF EXISTENTIAL COUNSELING

CONTENTS

PREFACE

When I speak of existential psychology or the existential viewpoint, I am not referring to a school of psychology which I would place side by side with other schools such as behaviorism, psychoanalysis, or the psychology of Alfred Adler. Rather the existential viewpoint embraces an attitude, an orientation of attention which I find, to some degree, represented in all schools of psychology and psychiatry. For example, this type of attention for basic phenomena is found in some of the writings of Tolman, the behaviorist; of Freud and Boss, the psychoanalysts; of Allport, Maslow, and Rogers, the humanist psychologists; and of May of the Alanson White Institute of Psychiatry.

I discover this specific turn of mind in these and other experts in my field when they pause from their empirical research and ask themselves: What is the structure and content of the experiences or perceptions which I am correlating, manipulating, or experimenting on? How would I make this perception explicit in such a way that my colleagues could affirm my qualitative description and agree upon it? How would this qualitative clarification of the objects which

[11]

I investigate influence the process of scientific investigation itself?

Asking himself such questions about certain perceptions which form the variables in his research, the scientist may discover, as I have, that men in other fields, such as phenomenological philosophy and cultural anthropology, have asked themselves similar questions about these perceptions, and from their findings, may arrive at a more comprehensive viewpoint. This is what is being attempted in the chapters to follow.

COUNSELING AND PSYCHOTHERAPY
AS HUMAN ENCOUNTER

IN this chapter I will attempt to make explicit what is implicit in the perception of one of the many variables which play a role in the research and practice of counseling and psychotherapy, namely, some aspects of the experience of encounter between the psychotherapist and his client.

To secure at least an initial and relative intersubjective agreement, I conducted this phenomenological research in dialogue with the descriptions given by some of the scholars who attempted the same, notably Binswanger, Buytendijk, DeGreeff, Heidegger, Kwant, Luijpen, Madinier, Marcel, May, Maslow, Moustakas, Nedoncelle, Rogers, and van den Berg. If my colleagues could affirm my descriptions or enrich them by correction or. expansion, this would mean one step more in the growth toward an intersubjective agreement on the qualites of certain basic phenomena which seem to take place in psychotherapy. I believe that the gradual establishment of such common knowledge would be beneficial for the orientation of research and praxis in counseling and psychotherapy as conducted in the various schools of psychology and psychiatry.

When we try to understand what counseling or psychotherapy really is, we should see it as primarily a human encounter. What is a truly human encounter? Everyone should understand immediately that an incidental crossing of someone else's path cannot be called a human encounter. An authentic human encounter always implies that I am, at least for some moments, totally present to a person, that I am fully with him. In a true encounter, I participate in the personal existence of another for whom I really care. To participate means literally to *take part in*. Thus encounter entails that I share the life of the other, the existence of the other, his way of being in the world.

Such human encounter may emerge at once as an unexpected gift in daily life. For example, I sit beside someone at a cafeteria table. We exchange the usual niceties that people are expected to exchange when they meet casual acquaintances. But then, all at once, the other speaks to me about an illness in his family, the sudden loss of a friend, or a painful experience that has occurred during the day. Something in his communication touches me and appeals to me. It moves me to answer him in a way that goes beyond the formal or incidental. It is as if the other dropped for a moment his social mask and invited me into the sanctuary of his inner life. I answer that appeal; I drop my own mask. Something grows between us, and a new reality is felt and expressed by both of us. What is this new reality? What is this new and vital relationship? What is this sudden creation of community?

Some may answer, "Nothing." Indeed, it seems nearly nothing. Still, something did happen. Something so real has emerged in our relationship that I will not be able to meet him again some day, or even the next day, without experiencing a more than casual acquaintanceship.

Sometimes a simple meeting of the eyes, the rendering of a service in a specific way, a little word, a change of tone, or a gesture of a hand is enough to evoke the experience of this hidden community of mutual concern between two human beings. They discover in and through these words and gestures each other's personality on a deep and very real level. Again we ask ourselves, "What does happen in such a meeting?"

Phenomenology attempts to make explicit what is spontaneously and implicitly experienced. It does not try to prove anything, but rather to manifest what is present in our experiences. Phenomenology is not eager to convince us of propositions by means of logical arguments or scientific experiments, although these are both very important and even necessary means of knowledge. Phenomenology, however, tries to help us before we start to reason logically or experimentally. This priority of phenomenology also applies to our understanding of human encounter. Once we know deeply what encounter really is, we can start to reason about its place in the framework of a personality theory or a therapeutic technique. But as long as we are not clear about the content of our spontaneous perception, we may be lost in a maze of ambiguous statements.

When we look again at the phenomenon of encounter, we realize, first of all, that the "we-experience" which emerged had a much deeper meaning and was pervaded by a much more genuine humanity and affection than is usually the case in other more routine meetings which fill our daily lives and are most often marked by indifference. In a genuine encounter, however, we experience real care for one another.

There is another remarkable difference between this "we-experience" and the routine meetings which I have with other people. Every person manifests a whole host of what can be called objective qualities. For example, I might have noticed that the other person was rather tall, had a loud voice, blue eyes, and an odd complexion. Meeting someone by chance in society, I tend to categorize him in this way, and to reduce his whole being to general predicates which in one form or another could be said about everyone. However, this experience of true encounter, strangely enough, makes such qualities fade into the background or shrink into insignificance. I am so taken in by his personal feelings, experiences, and attitudes that I become unaware of such accidental features as the color of his skin, the quality of his voice, and the movements of his hands. He is no longer one of the many people whose external profiles are carefully filed away in my memory. Even if I possess other information about him: his I.Q., his performance on an aptitude test, his age, and the social status of his family, I don't dwell on these facts when am experiencing a true human encounter. The personal seems to be so overwhelmingly present that it takes precedence over such measurable and objective characteristics. If I had reduced him to those peripheral qualities, there would not have grown between us the reality of encounter. If I saw him the next day, I would not experience him as this unique person for whom I really care, but as that man with the active hands, or the fellow with the I.Q. of 120, or that student with the sordid background, or the man with the booming voice. Such reductions of the unique person to a few of his objectivated or measured qualities make human encounter impossible. Therefore, as we will see later, it makes true counseling or psychotherapy an impossibility. Human encounter is the core of psychotherapy, the basis of change and growth by means of human relationships. It is the essence of cure in the deepest sense.

Authentic Therapeutic Encounter

In the situations which we have described, there is already present a beginning of what could be called real therapeutic care. There are, however, many situations which could be called true human encounter and which will manifest real care without being therapeutic. A boy scout who guides a blind man through traffic shows real care for this person. A stranger who takes pains to help me find my way downtown in a city unknown to me, and who goes literally out of his way to do this, manifests a genuine concern for me. A boy who loves a girl and expresses his love in many attentions truly encounters her and unmistakably cares for her. Yet, we could not say that all the manifestations of care in these situations are necessarily expressions of therapeutic care. The question with which we are faced is this: What is characteristic of the therapeutic encounter, or what are the conditions which make certain encounters therapeutic while others are not?

When I become therapeutically involved in the personal life of another human being, my commitment is an answer to some appeal of the *Other* which tells me that he needs me in a very personal way in some phase of his life and development. Many people make demands on me during a given day—on my energy, my time, my skills, or my interests. But these demands usually will not concern their personal growth and development. They may ask me for money, or to listen to their little stories or jokes, or to give them a hand in some work, or to explain some mathematical problem or a difficult selection of literature that they cannot understand. None of these amounts to a real personal appeal to help them grow in the area of human freedom where they are most themselves. This is why I can answer without involving the depth of my own being, without exposing the uniqueness of my own personality, or without the risk of being hurt because I have bared the deepest sensitivities of my own existence. I can hide and maintain my self-preoccupation while answering such daily demands which are of a more formal and passing nature. True, such an answer would grow in depth and richness if I were to engage more of my personality, but even if I do not do so, I can make a satisfactory response.

This, however, is very inadequate as a therapeutic response. When a person cries out in his despair about an anxiety which he cannot overcome, I cannot answer that appeal with the cool and exact information of how people can overcome such difficulties according to a manual of self-perfection or a textbook on psychology. If I reduce the gift of my person to such intellectual and generalized information, I am not fully and really present. I am only there as a factual intellect or an objective informant. The *appeal* of a whole person can be answered only by the *presence* of a whole person. Everything that is less is a betrayal of that appeal and an escape from the giving of one's self in the authentic therapeutic encounter.

Authentic Therapeutic Response to the Appeal of My Counselee

No matter how tenuous and hidden the appeal may be, it always contains the invitation to come out of myself. It is as if the other begs me to break through self-preoccupation and to escape my fascination with my egocentric world. The other seems to say, "Please leave your self-presence for a moment. Please be with .me, make my world for once the center of your attention, your sympathy, your kind understanding."

Why is it so difficult for me to hear the appeal of my counselee? To become a therapist means to go beyond my daily natural attitude of concentration on myself, that is, on my study of psychology, psychiatry, philosophy, or theology. It means to go beyond my convulsive anxious involvement in persons, books, things, and events that are relevant to my own well-being, my own career, and my own growth. This unconscious preoccupation with the impression that I make on my environment makes it difficult for me to understand, authentically, the real meaning of the appeal to me which may be hidden in a word, movement, story, or question of my counselee. During the counseling hour, I need more than my ears, eyes and far more than what I have learned in books of professional preparation for my work. What I need in the first place, and what is most difficult to obtain, is to break through my unconscious self-preoccupation.

One necessary condition and the initial base for counseling, then, is to *leave my self-centered world of daily involvement*. My counselee is anxious and at every moment on the point of retiring into himself. His hesitant expression of needs which he himself does not fully understand is neither violent or brusque, nor crystal clear. It is not an open attempt to conquer my interest, nor does it necessarily surprise, excite, or shock me. Especially in the beginning, it leaves an opening for a refusal. It is too delicate to force my attention. As long as I am occupied with my own conceptions about him and his case, obsessed with my half-conscious or unconscious needs to impress him by my understanding or fast and easy solutions, I will not understand the subtle shades of meaning in the words and movements of my counselee. Occupied in this way by personal desires and professional pride, I automatically excuse myself from the demands he makes on my unique presence.

One special form which this refusal of my real presence can take is to reduce myself to a professional role during the counseling hour. I am accustomed to playing a role in daily life, and as a counselor, I have other additional professional identifications. I may be a psychiatrist, psychologist, clergyman, educator, or psychodiagnostician, but I am of course far more than these societal roles. Nobody is merely a clergyman, a psychologist, a psychiatrist, or a teacher. My deepest being is not exhausted by these appearances; the core of my humanity if infinitely richer than any social manifestations. But as soon as I identify the whole of my being with only my professional role in society, I close myself off from the full, human appeal of the other. For I can understand him only when I am present to him as another fellow human being with untapped resources of human presence and understanding. Preoccupied with myself, with my appearance in daily society, and with the rules of making a formally perfect impression as the player of this role —all of these reduce immediately my ability to hear, to see, to sense, to understand, or to respond to the appeal of the counselee.

In order to answer this basic appeal, let us first consider what it is not. First of all, the appeal of my counselee ought not to be understood as the attraction of one or the other of his qualities or characteristics, such as his charming appearance, his beautiful voice, his poised behavior, his intelligent conversation, or his educational background. To be sure, such attractive qualities may make it interesting or desirable for me to be with him, but this attraction would be meaningless if my client did not have engaging manners or were no longer to manifest them in the therapy sessions. Such qualities and manners call forth only a superficial desire to be *with* my counselee, while therapeutic response and care indicates more my stable and consistent will to be *for* my client. The therapist who really cares understands that the physical, emotional, moral, or cultural qualities of his client do not matter very much in the counseling relationship. They fade into the background to make room for those more personal and unique qualities in which the client is more than a case history, more than the influences of his past and present environment. Authentic therapeutic response is not motivated by the attractions and signs of promise in the client. None of these can explain why the counselor is able to commit himself wholly and unconditionally to the growth of his patient.

Neither, as we have seen, can the appeal of the client to the counselor be understood as identical with a concrete request that he happens to express during the therapy hour. A specific demand is never, as such, the appeal of a person, as a whole, to be totally with and for him. If it contains a real appeal, a demand for the solution of a problem or even for the interpretation of a dream or symptom, it is always more than what it seems to be. Such a demand may contain nothing more than the presentation to the therapist of a factual problem or symptom which needs explanation or interpretation. However, even though I satisfy concretely and prosaically this demand, the counselee may depart unsatisfied because I have answered only the appearance of his question and not the far deeper cry which underlies the simple, factual presentation of his problem. He will leave me without, perhaps, being able to explain why I have disillusioned him; on the surface, everything *seemed* all right. He presented his problem to me and I gave him a neat, logical, clear-cut answer, according to the best textbooks and authors dealing with this matter, but he is still as lonely, confused, and anxious as he was before he entered my study for an hour of counseling.

The client who comes to me for therapeutic counseling is not a person who has a problem or request but a person who is an appeal. This appeal to my presence, expressed in an awkward and deceptive way as a concrete problem, goes far beyond this—to the mysterious core of his personality. This unique, personal core itself is an appeal to me as a full and unique human being to participate in his deepest being. could translate this appeal into the simple word "Please be with and for me."

Thus, a second necessary condition for all fruit, counseling is that the counselor hears the appeal of the counselee. This does not mean that it is necessary that he clearly and reflectively knows that he hears it. Such reflection may even disturb my spontaneous presence to the core of my patient. This appeal is the counselee's hidden prayer, his silent begging, his unspoken cry to go out of my self-centered daily preoccupation with my own world, and to be willing to sustain the unique and embattled core of his confused and painful existence, to be willing to strengthen by my presence this free core of his being, to increase his free personality.

To do so I should really care for my client and be in sympathy with him without falling into the trap of misunderstanding such terms. In daily life, care and sympathy frequently mean sentimental indulgence, unrealistic leniency, or spineless compliance with all the needs and desires of another. Such sentimental indulgence differs widely from authentic therapeutic care. The wishes of the client, whether they are expressed or not, may be arbitrary, unrealistic, out of tune with his true destiny, and inhibitory of real growth. Many of his desires may be impulses, isolated from the core of his real, unique self. As a good therapist, I should try to fully understand and sense such wishes, and not foster a repression or denial of this awareness. However, if the therapist's understanding of sympathy and care is wrong, he may feel inclined not only to sympathize with such tendencies but to encourage their execution, even if they are contrary to the real growth of the person.

One way to show a misconception of sympathy is for the counselor to manifest a warm affection for the other in ways that, I find, delight me personally. In that case, my care and sympathy is not so much a real love and concern for his growth but a subtle kind of self-preoccupation. Unconsciously, I want to realize myself in my client. I hope that his growth will be a testimony to my excellent view of existence. On the other hand, I may be inclined to make the other an extension of my own individuality or of the common character of a group of people with whom I am deeply identified. Every sign in his communication or behavior of a growing identification with my style of life evokes in me a visible increase in care and sympathy. This false type of sympathy goads and directs the client away from his own individuality, from his own initiative, and from his own unique self-actualization. It is again a form of not involving myself in the world of my counselee, but involving him in my world; that is, making him a part of my situation. This type of care and affection is poisoned by my self-centeredness and is severely harmful to the client. Often, there is no therapeutic care whatsoever. This situation reminds us of so-called loving parents who force their children against their own inclinations to play the role which has been chosen for them and then lavish praise when they do well.

The Counselor's Relationship to the Counselee

Authentic therapeutic care has nothing to do with this attempt to dominate, control, and direct the life of my client according to my own individual project of existence. The authentic counselor who really cares

will treat the counselee as a free subject and try to
constitute him as such. In this connection, we could
speak about the *reservedness of therapeutic concern.*
Reservedness on the part of counselor or psychotherapist expresses an immense respect for the unique responsibility of the client. This respect is essential; its
lack would destroy the therapy situation. The authentic therapist respectfully participates in the counselee's
way of being in the world in order to help him to
become more fully what he potentially is. His reservedness implies attitudes which prevent him from inter-
fering arbitrarily in the world of his client.

True therapeutic concern is, at the least, an implicit
awareness of the inalienableness of my client's life. The
good therapist is delighted when the patient meets
more and more his own destiny. In this manner, and
in no other sense, am I called to counsel him because I
counsel him in order to enable him to actualize himself in his world, in his life, and in his unique bodily
situation, all of which are very different from mine.

The body situation and the life situation contain
for my counselee the factual realities which are points
of departure for the free actualization of the special
possibilities characteristic of his world. My therapeutic
presence should enable him to give meaning and direction to his existence. The realistic limitations of
human fulfillment can always be pointed out by a careful estimation of the factual environment, including
both our own bodily limitations and those given us in

our social culture. For example, each type of counseling directs itself primarily toward one or the other concrete life situations in which the counselee finds it difficult to discover or to actualize his personal destiny in a harmonious, well-integrated way. There is psychiatric therapy, psychological therapy, vocational counseling, religious counseling, rehabilitation counseling, and marriage counseling. A full understanding of each of these special life situations may require special training, experience, and study. But underlying all possible forms of therapeutic counseling is the fundamental attitude of authentic therapeutic care which fosters in my client a personal looking for his own way in the world, his own destiny.

The therapist, therefore, participates in the free self-actualization of his client in the light of the claims of reality; authentic counseling excludes everything that could inhibit or destroy the free actualization of the self in the light of the life vocation and the authentic life situation. Therefore, if tendencies, wishes, and inclinations make impossible the real growth of the client, then the therapist will refuse to encourage their execution. For example, the acting out of suicidal wishes or of sexual desires in regard to children cannot be fostered by the therapist. Their very fulfillment would lift the client out of the reality of his life situation and would, consequently, seriously inhibit his possibility of growth in responsibility toward reality.

We may now want to ask, What is my relationship to the counselee as manifested in my therapeutic care? I have seen that therapeutic care desires the freedom of my client, and therefore makes me, in a certain sense, defenseless because it inspires infinite confidence and a limitless trust. Therapy is self-surrender in the sense that the counselor or therapist surrenders to his client. This complete trust and self-surrender implies the full and defenseless presence of the therapist to his client. The very trust which I give without limits to my client, revealed in my unconditional therapeutic care, is in and by itself an appeal to the counselee to be concerned as I am concerned.

It is not the desire or attempt of the therapist to profit by, or reap benefits from the affection, sympathy, or care which he manifests for the other. The authentic counselor considers it impossible to strive for the fulfillment of his own needs or the promotion of his own growth and at the same time keep pure his therapeutic involvement. When a counselee discovers that the counselor cares for him only in order to make money, or to grow in experience, or to become self-actualized, he cannot have the feeling that he is really accepted for himself. Moreover, the appeal of the counselee is not a subtle plea for my domination. The good counselor wants the counselee *himself* to choose this right way and *himself* to avoid the other harmful direction. While authentic counseling implies my being at the disposal of the other, it does not entail my giving into the temptation to protect him for the sake of my own success.

What emerges seems to indicate a polarity in the life of the good counselor. Increasingly, he breaks through his narrow self-involvement, and this effort enables him to be more and more sensitive to the appeal of his clients. These appeals in turn enable him to go more and more out of himself, and as he transcends himself to be more sensitive to the next invitation to be with and for his counselee. In this way, the life of the good therapist is like a widening spiral. Starting out humbly as a man who has a hard time breaking through his self-preoccupation, he grows increasingly to an openness, participation, and presence. His life is continuously enriched, expanded, and deepened. This is the great and beautiful reward of the life of counseling (though counseling can never be practiced for the sake of this reward because this very search itself would be a form of self-preoccupation and would diminish or destroy the goal he sought, namely, the full presence to the other).

As a beginning counselor, the appeal of the counselee reveals to me a totally new, perhaps unsuspected, dimension of my own existence. I am called to realize myself as a full human being *for* the counselee. His call announces to me that it is part of my destiny to be for him a full understanding presence. Through my counselee, I become at once aware of the meaninglessness of my egocentricism and glib professionalism. Without him, I would be bound by success and status to imprison myself in my little professional and administrative world, totally incapable of realizing myself as a human being. The appeal of the counselee truly helps me to free myself; this is his great gift to me. In turn, his appeal demands an answer of the real me to the begging, "Please be with and for me." This begging is an appeal for the best that I am, an appeal for being together with him. On the other hand, "Be satisfied when I give you what I *have*"—diagnostic logical advice, an explanation, a sharp and surprising interpretation, a prescription of drugs or exercises—means that I shut myself off in my world, hoping that the other will not disturb me again. I remain alone as the expert, the doctor, the professor, the administrator, or the diagnostician—and the other remains far away, the interesting case history.

Being a good counselor is therefore paradoxical in many ways: I exist not only for my counselee; I exist, also, for myself. I am, also, a presence to myself. Even when I am fully present to my counselee, I remain an "I," a "selfness." But I remain only an "I," a "selfness," in my fusion with the "not-self." For being human is a paradox of selfness and transcendence. The paradox of being man is even more dramatic in the therapy situation. Being a counselor is my being at the disposal of my counselee and totally dedicated to the unique personality which my client is. On the other hand, in the giving of myself and in the surrender of myself to my counselee, my real, authentic self is revealed, actualized and expanded. This real self is the best in me, my authentic "I" which is at the disposal of my client, not the functional or social "me."

This insight leads immediately to the question: Is my implicit appeal in the care of the counselee perhaps my silent supplication to him to give me the possibility of fulfilling my own humanity? Is a disinterested therapist really possible? Can I ever want something good for the counselee without wanting this good at the same time as a form of self-actualization and self-fulfillment for myself?

Therapeutic care is a most interesting case of this eternal human dilemma. For authentic therapeutic care wants in *every* case the interest of the client. On the other hand, it is impossible for me as a counselor to forego the fact that my therapeutic care as a full turning toward my client is at the same time the fulfillment of my deepest being, understood as a being-towards-the-other. However, this does not mean that the actualization of my own humanity is the sole motivation for the loving care of my counselee. The opposite is true. In therapeutic care I actualize myself only under one condition: namely, that this self-actualization, this growth in human perfection, is not the motivation of my counseling or therapy. Imagine for a moment that my client were thanking me for my care, understanding, and therapy and that I were waving it away by saying that it was merely a question of fulfilling my own humanity, of becoming perfect, or of gaining self-actualization. It would be immediately clear to my client that he is not cared for in an authentic sense but only in the interest of my personal growth.

It may very well be that secret egocentric motivations permeate my attempt to be a good counselor. As long as this is the case, my therapeutic presence will be less effective. The client may not know why, but he feels less understood, less at home and at ease with me. There is an invisible curtain between us which prevents full openness on both sides. Even where I counsel because it is the right and honorable thing for me to do when a person comes to me in need, even then this motivation is not counselee-directed but in some subtle way self-directed. The feeling that I should fulfill this obligation as a gentleman still implies a concern for myself. Each such self-centered motivation diminishes the effectiveness of the counseling relationship. Sometimes concern for my goodness is so deeply rooted in my background that I myself may need psychotherapy, in order to become clearly aware of it and to transcend it. This concern for perfection may spoil not only the relationship between a psychotherapist and a patient but also the relationship between a teacher and a student who comes to him with a personality problem, or between a religious counselor and a counselee who asks him about his religious mode of existence. When the teacher or the religious counselor is influenced deeply by the idea that he should counsel in order to grow in self-actualization or in his profession, the counseling relationship is vitiated. There is, in the literal sense, a barrier between the counselor and the counselee that cannot be taken away by any amount of advice or sympathetic verbalization. The only way in which this relationship can be fulfilled is by transcending such self-preoccupied motivations and really responding to the appeal of my client.

The Counselee's Response to the Counselor

As we have seen, the authentic counselor wants to affirm the unique personality and the spontaneous initiative of his counselee; he wants him to grow in his own independent being. But this desire can bear fruit only when the counselee ratifies my therapeutic attempt by his own consent to my desire for him. Therapeutic care does not want to force or to impose. What is more, as soon as the counselor tries to overpower the counselee, if only by suggestion, then his activity is no longer therapeutic care. Counseling can only become authentic by means of the free consent and cooperation of the other. If he does not consent freely, all the improvement that he shows as a result of my clever suggestions will not be a real improvement, though it may help him to adjust more smoothly to the demands of his community. His external changes in this case will not be rooted in his own free insight, but in my insight. I may have brainwashed him by means of syllogisms, interpretations, the seductive promise of kindness, and the overwhelming impact of my personality; but, instead of helping him to become free, I have robbed him of his freedom, stolen his initiative, paralyzed his personal sensitivity for reality. No matter how I may have ornamented him with splendid external behavior or with perfect adaptation to his community, it cannot compensate for my having taken away his own basic insight and freedom. Without this freedom, no virtue, regardless of its splendor, can be his virtue; no charitable adjustment, regardless of its smoothness, can be his charity. Thus, we see that therapeutic care reaches its aim only if the counselee freely ratifies my desire for him to choose freely that which is good and true in his life.

Even though the counselor may have to shut off certain ways of being in the world for the counselee, his desire will be that the counselee take it upon *himself* to avoid such ways. It is not enough for therapeutic care to make it literally impossible for the counselee to harm himself or others. No, my appeal as a counselor to my counselee is that he develop the power to see for himself and to experience for himself that his way cannot lead to the fulfillment of his destiny. "See for yourself, and realize in freedom your own being, your own destiny, and your own happiness. Never do it merely because I suggest it, or because I like it. Never do it because you like me, for all such reasons lie outside your existence. Your goodness should grow out of your own openness to reality as revealed in your unique life situation." The only fruit for which I may be legitimately hopeful is that the counselee will exist authentically and lose any dependence he may have on me, that he may find himself as his own initiator of life.

Thus a ratification by my counselee means that he should care as much for himself as I care for him. But should therapeutic love be mutual? As we have seen, for successful counseling it is necessary for my client to accept my being at his disposal. However, this does not mean that the counselee ought to be interested in me with the same intensity as I care for him. It is unrealistic for the counselor to expect the demonstration of such care and love in the counselee, for it requires lifelong development to attain the ability of surrendering oneself to another so that he may use you for his own growth without feeling obliged to give anything back. In the counselor it is precisely this unconditional surrender to the counselee which enables the latter to use the counselor without the risk of becoming so dependent emotionally on the counselor that he loses his freedom. In the nature of the therapeutic situation, the counselor is the fully matured being capable of this formidable gift of total self-giving, while the client remains the being in whom this is still only a possibility. Therefore, the initial counseling relationship is unilateral.

This unilateral and total gift of oneself makes for one of the differences between the counseling relationship and the love relationship as we know it in daily life. It would be impossible, so it seems, for a human being to maintain this attitude of unilateral total self-surrender to the other for long periods of time. For this reason, the therapeutic counselor must always limit himself to certain fixed periods of counseling relationship. Otherwise he would not be able to maintain this attitude because of irritation, impatience, or tension. These would grow and show themselves if the hours of counseling were too prolonged and would thus harm the effectiveness of the relationship.

The authentic meaning of my being destined as a counselor for the counselee is difficult to define. His appeal is not a clearly formulated demand, and my answer is not a logical compliance. The answer to the appeal of the counselee is an answer given to him as a unique and responsible person, the source of his own world of meaning and value. As a free and responsible person, he gives continual meaning and value to his symptoms, problems, and life situations. As another "I," as a "self," the counselee has to find his own way in the world and to unveil in his lifetime his own destiny. He has to live his own unique history. His appeal to me means that he invites me to will his free, unique, responsible personality, to present him with the possibility of existing in his own responsible way, to join in his freedom and responsibility, and to accept and sustain his free discovery of meaning in his world. He appeals to me to make it my care and concern that he may be what he is, that he may become what he can be best. Therapeutic care is to will the existence of the counselee as a responsible and free *you* who finds his own destiny. It is my commitment to the autonomous development of that "you."

CHAPTER II

THE FREEDOM AND CREATIVITY
OF THE THERAPEUTIC RELATIONSHIP

THE lines which gradually become visible in our phenomenology of therapeutic care all converge on one point: namely, you, the client; you, the counselee. In a very deep sense the therapy relationship is only about this "you." Otherwise, as we shall now see, it would lose its authenticity and might even be destroyed completely. Therapeutic care becomes possible only when I am sensitive to the unique personality of my counselee, when I no longer consider my counselee a compilation of symptoms, or diagnostic characteristics, as a textbook syndrome, or an "interesting case." As we have seen, the appeal to me is the counselee in his totality and not one or the other of his expressed demands. Therapeutic care may be succinctly summarized by saying that the motivation of counseling is "you." I care for you because you are lovable, and you are essentially lovable because you are you.

This "you" does not have a merely neutral meaning of being the object of my address; I mean rather that I meet you in your singular uniqueness. It is not possible to meet this unique "you" by means of the methods of the positive sciences. The positive sciences will accept as meaningful only what can be expressed by means of measurement. But, I cannot recognize anything I think of as being you in the "you" of measurements. The only way in which I can discover you in your uniqueness is in experiencing you; this experience will only become truly mine when I really care for you as you. It cannot be taught, explained, measured, or described. Every such description presupposes the experience. My experience of you is the same as my love for you; it must be actual. If I have never experienced love in my life, then reading heavy volumes about it will not help me to understand it. Phenomenologically expressed, my disposition or attitude as a counselor reveals to me what my client, as a unique person in this world, really is. A positive approach can only reduce the unique "you" of my client to a summation of psychological and physical qualities, or to a descriptive list of his symptoms or his character. This approach looks for the unique "you" of my client in a filled-out questionnaire, in the familiar case history file, where he is diagnosed and categorized. But the "you" of my client is essentially beyond categorization, beyond diagnosis, and beyond interpretations.

This does not mean, of course, that therapeutic care need be only a subjectivistic statement about my counselee; that I, the counselor, am no longer able to determine that my patient is, e.g., aggressive, immature, hostile, or overdependent. On the contrary, the counselor who really cares see not only these symptoms but reaches out to their deepest roots in the core of the personality of his counselee. Existential therapeutic care enables him to see both the symptoms and the subjective "you" and to interrelate them as a whole of the client's being. It makes impossible a reduction of the counselee to a series of pathological categories or test scores. Authentic therapeutic care keeps the therapist present to that which is more than the symptoms, test profiles, and problems of adjustment. Therapeutic care enables the counselor to go beyond any diagnostic category. Recognition of this fact is necessary because the person finds himself in the world in a unique way and no diagnostic category can do justice to this.

Let us now penetrate further into the attitude of therapeutic care. We have already stressed that I, the counselor, actively turn toward my counselee. But now we would like to delineate this turning toward as a creative movement. In order to see that therapeutic care is really creative, I have to grasp the meaning of creativity. Every time that I am open for reality, reality appears to me in new and surprising ways. In a very deep sense, I let reality be for me. I allow reality to reveal itself as it is. I respect and accept the manifestations of reality. However, while it is true that I am somehow active in this "letting-be" of goodness, truth, and beauty for me, I am also passive because this understanding of reality implies sensitivity and receptivity. Therefore, a knowledge which is simply a "letting-be" of reality cannot be called creative in the full sense. Let us take another example. When a carpenter makes a table, he is far more than merely sensitive and receptive. Not only does he understand the meaning of a tree but he makes a table out of the wood of the tree. In other words, he establishes a new meaning, creates something that was not yet there in that form. The same could be said about the work of the poet. When a poet writes a real piece of poetry, it is because he uses the words of his language in a new and surprising way, creating something that was not yet present in this form. The same can be applied to a musical composition, a painting, or a sculpture. The therapeutic encounter is creative in the same way. My active turning toward my client really makes him be in a new way.

Therapeutic Encounter and Modes of Being

To understand this in its proper context, I must first realize that not only the therapy encounter, but every encounter, makes the other be in some way. The way in which I make the other be is very much determined by the kind of encounter we have. Take a simple daily situation. Two men meet each other in a bar and the first phase of this encounter may be a friendly formality. One man expresses some kindness to the other and the other answers him kindly. Further talk ensues, and for each new pleasant expression of sympathy and companionship there is evoked a counterexpression of interest in the other. Later, the two, as a result of these increasingly kind exchanges, are at ease with each other. Then, perhaps, one man says something about a current political situation that has lots of people stirred up, and says it in such a way as to leave no doubt in his hearer's mind which side he is on. The other person, let us say, holds the opposite opinion, and as a result he feels offended and threatened, and may well answer this challenge by an equally forceful argument of his own, perhaps in a voice a shade louder than his challenger's was. The other responds in kind, and before either of them realizes it, the friendly meeting is a heated debate soon to turn into a swinging brawl. If we look closely at the development of this encounter, we will see how the attitude of each man at every moment created a new mode of being in the other. The two persons in this example started out as superficial acquaintances. Then they created a companionship of two friendly people. They created and reinforced this attitude in one another. After that they switched to creating an encounter of heated discussants; and finally, they created each other in the mode of boisterous fighters. The important thing to see is that they did so "by" and "through" the other. They really and truly made each other be, first as casual acquaintances, then as sympathetic friends, next as heated discussants, and finally as boisterous fighters. We are so used to making each other be in daily life that we are seldom aware of the fact that we can make the other be in a specific way.

It is totally impossible for me to think about any mode of being in which I am perfectly *alone*. All my modes of being in the world are influenced by the existence of others. Others make me be, and I make others be. The reality which I am is not an isolated reality independent of others. I can only understand myself as born from the other, or as nourished and educated by the other, as speaking the language the other speaks, as wearing clothing that is created by others, or as having customs generated by many others before me. A mother is a mother through her child. A Negro is only a Negro when there are whites. An asocial family is only completely so when left alone or rejected by society. Someone may object and say that one can declare a Negro is a Negro or a Jew is a Jew without whites and anti-Semites. However, this is a misunderstanding because it presupposes that being Jewish or Negro is merely a biological conception. This conception does not take into account the being of a Negro and a Jew. A Jew is not a Jew and a Negro is not a Negro in the same way that a chair is a chair or a tree is a tree. The chair or the tree does not know or care about being a chair or a tree. But a human being who is a Negro or a Jew is very much conscious of his being a Negro or a Jew. He takes a position toward his being a Jew or a Negro. What makes man distinct from chairs or trees is that he always takes an attitude toward his mode of being. He is always giving meaning to his own mode of being.

However, the meaning which a Negro or a Jew gives to his being a Negro or a Jew is dependent for a great part on the way in which other people treat him. Therefore, the treatment of a Jew as a Jew and of a Negro as a Negro by the others in the encounter with the others makes him really be a Negro or a Jew, creates him as such. A small infant who is colored may only be created as a colored child at the moment he is treated differently from people who are not colored. This treatment makes him be in a different way, makes him think and act in a different way. It was the encounter which created him "Negro." In all these examples, it may be clear that I am what I am largely through the other and that the others are what they are largely through me.

Now, we will apply this to the specific nature of therapeutic care. We ask ourselves in what way can I make the other be through my attitude of therapeutic care? In what way does my therapeutic care influence the way of life of my counselee? My therapeutic care makes the counselee be in a way no other encounter (except the love encounter) makes him be. Encounters which are not encounters of love or of therapeutic care result in social classifications which are imposed on and experienced by the other during such encounters. When the colored child, in his encounter with white people, experiences what it means to be colored in a predominantly white society, he becomes more or less determined by this experience. It is a fact, a social fact, which categorizes him and hems him in. The same sort of thing happens when a test diagnostician has a professional encounter with the person who is to take a test. The outcome of the test, such as an I.Q., or a profile of aptitudes, makes the tested person be in a certain way: namely as the person who is conscious of the limitations of his "intelligence" or of a range of "skills." Other examples are the writing of one's case history by a social worker, or the careful enumeration of one's physical and psychological symptoms by a medical expert. All such descriptions do indeed indicate a certain number of more or less valid facts about me. They certainly make me aware of these facts and therefore they make me be in relation to these concrete data. I am quite a different person when I leave the office of my doctor after he has told me that I have cancer, diabetes, or an ulcer than I was before I learned about these physical facts. The same is true of a counselee of mine who "learned" about "himself" in meetings with experts such as diagnostic psychologists and medical doctors.

However, my counselee, as unique personal "I," is not identical with these facts. Such symptoms, assets, and deficits are only a starting point for the ultimate realization of possibilities which are implied in the given data. My counselee is freedom, he is the possibility of initiative, he is the source of meaning and existence. To be sure, these facts when valid indicate certain broad limits within which he can grow and actualize his capacities; they can helpfully eliminate certain orientations of actualization. A counselee with an accurately measured I.Q. of 90 is unlikely to become a quantum physicist of great renown, nor will a deaf person become a famous opera singer. However, within the limits of one's factual orientation the possibilities of self-actualization are inexhaustible.

How one chooses to grow within these limits depends upon one's freedom, upon the independent stand which one takes in the world; and it is the therapeutic encounter which can grant my client this freedom, making it possible for him to be not only within but over and beyond his factual limitations and determinations. It makes him experience his factual determinations no longer as unchangeable objects but as possibilities by means of which he can actualize himself. This does not mean, of course, that my counselee was not a free, unique personality before my therapeutic care. My counselee is basically a free person, and not a thing, even when his freedom is stifled or crushed under the weight of his neurotic anxiety and guilt feelings, his destructive habits, his overdependency, his compulsions, depression, and paranoid attitudes. He is never a stone or any other thing, but always basically free. It is precisely the radical nature of this freedom which makes psychotherapy possible.

Man's freedom has roots that are in his very nature as man. It cannot be totally eradicated by circumstances, no matter how severely it is stifled under the stiff iron mesh of neurotic patterns. However, we may also use the expression "free, unique personality" to indicate the person in the fullness of being, when he has reached the top level of freedom. His freedom is such that he is able to give complete fulfillment to each of the facts that go toward making up his personality. His freedom stretches so widely into all corners of his life that he is able to turn each obstacle or adversity into a positive personal value. In freedom, he becomes able to experience his very illnesses in such a way that they help him grow.

My client, limited at first by his neurotic controls, after a period of therapy, reaches the fullness of freedom and is able to affirm himself as a source of initiative within his life situation. We do not find freedom in mere physical mobility, for we can even speak of freedom of a prisoner. As a counselor in a prison, it is the aim and meaning of my existence to make the prisoner free, not in a physical sense, but in a far more essential and fundamental way: namely, the freedom of giving a meaning to all his limitations which enables him to soar psychologically beyond those walls, and to actualize himself in a meaningful way hitherto unknown to him when he faced the bars of his restricting situation. By my therapeutic care, I participate in the free, unique core of his being which is hampered by his inhibitions. Therefore, in the core of his being, he is no longer a lonely, threatened individual faced with the responsibility of devising his project of existence against the tremendous odds in his present personality. Now he may open up to his potential reality and face his limitations because I am with him. I am present there where he is as much or more than all his indecisions and his fears. I am presenting him, as it were, to himself. I enable his real self to emerge and to take hold of his potentialities and limitations.

Therapeutic Care Is Creative

The therapeutic relationship is fructifying and creative because therapeutic care creates a new "you" in the patient. Its aim is not to fashion a person in accordance with one or the other theory of personality, but to help bring about a free, unique person who will then feel, think, and act as an "I," and not as a disciple of any school of psychology or psychiatry. The force of my authentic, therapeutic love and concern leads to the moment in which anxiety-evoking situations lose their insurmountability for my client. My authentic, therapeutic sympathy enables him to emerge as the relaxed and flexible master of his life situation. Therapy thus enables the person to actualize himself on a level and to a degree which he never would have reached if he had been left alone.

This awareness of being no longer alone in the depth of his being is perhaps the clearest manifestation of the creativity of the therapy relationship. Therapeutic love and concern creates a "we," a companionship which is experienced as totally different from the "we" of daily social situations. It is nearly impossible to describe this "we-experience," which is characteristic of the best hours of authentic counseling. When we try to express it, we fall back on such terms as "fullness," "fulfillment," "full presence," and "joy of being." It resolves itself into the fact that therapeutic care makes my client experience the joy and the vigor of being a new "I."

Also, the world of my client undergoes a re-creation through the therapeutic encounter. The world of the client is a correlate of his unique, free individuality, and it is a system of meanings. The meaning of reality for him is determined by his free attitudes. However, his true personal attitudes were not awakened before the therapeutic encounter; they were smothered by neurotic anxieties which conjured up for him a desolate, frightening world, a world which choked and oppressed him. However, as I participate lovingly in his deepest, free individuality, I participate also in the world of meaning which he creates. Therefore, he experiences in my concern for his own freedom the truth that I want the real and personal world for him.

Moreover, I, as a therapist, am also part of this world which the counselee experiences. I, as a therapist, am a living respect and concern for my counselee as freedom. I am the continuous absence of any forcing or overpowering of the free and unique development of my counselee. This will gradually lead to a situation in which the world shows the counselee its mildest face.

Many patients have had to meet the world always at its most crude and hateful. Parents withheld from them real love. Fathers and mothers might have been preoccupied with the factual assets and deficits of their children, with their correct or incorrect behavior, with their success or failure in school, or with their deportment in the eyes of the neighbors. They did not permit themselves to be present to the individual core of their children in freedom, and to show that concern that lies far beyond all mere lists of their factual determinations. As a result, such children have never found themselves. They are able only to experience themselves as collections of assets and deficiencies or of successes and failures. They perceive the world as a place in which one is acceptable only as an external failure or success, and they perceive people as liking or condemning according to one's external conformity or rebellion. The world for these loveless children becomes a hell in which they are tortured by the constant and usually unfulfilled need to be accepted; so they hope desperately to escape destruction by being seen as beyond reproach in the eyes of another. They experience the world as a place where one can never hope to be accepted for what he is. Their very anxious conformity to the wishes of others, the very compulsion to please others, makes them lose the freedom they need for wholeness. They become the parrots of society or one of its subcultures, the slaves of the group opinion.

The very absence of a unique, free stand invites sadistic control and enslavement by the people around them. The suppressed, unique "I" in turn develops a deep hate, a limitless rage against the oppressors which further paralyzes growth and movement. I, as a therapist, by my respectful fostering of this oppressed unique core of the personality can break this monotonous circle of false perception and experience. My presence to the suppressed uniqueness of my counselee may lead first to the eruption of stored up hostility, which is directed toward me as the only person against whom he can dare to live out these personal feelings. Nevertheless, I will maintain my attitude of unshakable respect and love for the unique, independent source of initiative which the person is, even though it reveals itself first in this negative way.

But the therapeutic care of the psychological counselor can only be creative when the counselee accepts freely this loving concern. The "yes" of the counselee is necessary to ratify the therapeutic concern of the counselor and make this fruitful and creative. The psychotherapist wants the freedom and transcedence of the counselee, and so he can only want the counselee to consent freely to the loving care which is offered to him. Therapeutic care for the patient amounts to wanting his *freedom*. When the counselee does simply what he is told because of the fact that to him the counselor is an expert or "sees through him" or "is such a nice fellow," the subtle process of enlargement to his freedom is stillborn. Therapeutic care is only fertile when the person himself who has to grow chooses to do so. For this reason, the approach of psychotherapy must be entirely different from that of medicine. Psychotherapeutic influence is an interchange between two human beings in which both are active and in which both participate. Without this free participation by the counselee, psychotherapy cannot be. This "yes" of the counselee is his gift to the counselor.

All that we have said also makes it clear that we can never describe therapy in a literal cause-effect sense in the way we describe the effectiveness of a medical expert who treats a physical injury or disease. A broken leg can be healed and internal illness can be arrested even if the patient is unconscious. Medical science directs itself to physiological factual aspects of the patient. By its nature, medical science confines, restricts, prescribes, and manipulates its patients. Psychotherapeutic treatment, however does the very opposite; it aims at the freedom of the patient. It does not approach the heart as a diseased organ susceptible to chemical cures, but as an aspect of the client's total world. It does not attempt to cure a single symptom, whether biological or psychological. It organizes its attention to influence the free attitude of a patient toward his ailment. For this reason a strict medical therapy and a strict psychotherapy of the same person may complement each other to benefit the patient. This is especially true when these opposite types of treatment are offered by experts in each field who do not confound the two different types of treatment. The two totally different attitudes must be kept distinct while the practitioners work together in order to benefit each of the two modes of being of the patient. The medical practitioner should show some psychological concern for his patient, but it is not his primary task to foster the growth of freedom of the unique core of the patient. His primary concentration is on certain factual, physiological and physical states of his patient. He will appreciate, however, that the inner attitude which the patient in freedom takes toward his physical disabilities may influence the process of healing.

CHAPTER III

FREEDOM, HUMAN WILL AND
THE AFFIRMATION OF REALITY
IN THE THERAPEUTIC RELATIONSHIP

EXISTENTIAL psychology sees man as living in a human world; therefore, when my counselee enters my room, he is not alone, but rather brings with him a whole world. My little room is crowded, as it were, by a whole universe in which my client breathes, perceives, and lives; for nothing exists for any human being that does not have a certain meaning for him. The world for us is really what people, events, and things mean to us. The world for my counselee is that which all things mean to him. And it is important to realize that I don't know beforehand what they mean to him. I cannot predict his world with accuracy. I cannot find it in a learned textbook. The only way to discover it is for me to be totally open to what my client will reveal to me about the world in which he lives, providing I am deeply respectful, loving, and understanding. What is more, my counselee himself may not yet be aware in a reflective way about what the world really means to him. Therefore, if he can really speak out in the therapy relationship, not only I but also he himself may discover in what way he lives in the world.

As we have seen before, my therapeutic care should make my client free. It is basically an event of liberation. What does freedom mean in respect to my client's world of meaning? It seems clear that the universe of meaning within which my counselee moves cannot be called free if he himself does not in some way decide that his world should have this meaning in his life; for reality has an inexhaustible possibility of meaning. For example, a child can experience the building blocks of his playhouse as toys to play with until his little sister annoys him. At that moment a whole new meaning of the building blocks may be revealed to him. He experiences them at once as projectiles to be thrown at his sister. This new meaning of the same object does not make untrue the former meaning. Later on, when his mother forces him into the bathtub, he may unveil a totally new aspect of the reality of the building blocks. They keep afloat, and you can use them as little ships which relieve the ordeal of having to wash yourself so many times a week. In such a way man's existential world of meaning expands by an increasing number of discoveries of reality.

However, man may decide freely to limit his openness for reality to only one of its manifold appearances. For example, a little boy who does not feel loved, accepted, and appreciated may develop a tremendous aggression and hostility. We can even imagine that his angry feelings are so vehement that he is unable to see any toy as a toy. He experiences prevailingly only one of the possible meanings of his toys: namely, that they can be used as weapons to hurt other people or to force other people to the awareness that one is around and kicking. In that case, he becomes fixated on a one-sided meaning of the world. And at the same time his painful experiences with his parents may sensitize him to the negative, loveless, and hostile aspects of humanity and not allow him to be open for the cordial, appreciative, and helpful aspects which human beings may manifest to him. In this case we must say that this one-sided world of meaning is not freely and consciously decided upon by him. He may not even be aware that he lives in such a gloomy world while he could live in a world in which the light side also would appear.

This world of meaning is not freely chosen. It is the outcome of traumatic experiences which influence his life without his being able to do anything about it. The tragic thing is that the meaning of our world is not without influence on our behavior. On the contrary, our behavior is a response to what the world means to us. The little boy for whom the world and people are frightening and full of threat will necessarily behave in a suspicious, anxious, or defiant way. Soon his behavior is conditioned by the meaning which he perceives in his environment. In that sense his behavior is determined by his perception of the world in the same manner as his perception of the world is determined by his traumatic past. We cannot say that his free, unique core of being had a chance to grow and develop. It has been crushed, as it were, by the one-sided meaning which his life history imposed on him without his consent. His behavior is the unavoidable answer to this lopsided appearance of reality.

The Counselee's World of Meaning Uncovered By His Freedom

Counseling means the making free of such a person. Now, I can only reach that goal by awakening his unique personality, by evoking and re-creating him as a free and alive source of meaning and by allowing him to experience himself, in the counseling situation, as an independent unveiling of sense and meaning in his world. To be sure, when he becomes free in his evaluation of reality, his behavior may again become conditioned by the new meaning which he discovers in his life situation. However, this conditioning happens as a result of an openness for meanings which are not imposed on his freedom, but are uncovered by his freedom. Moreover, his increase in freedom will enable him to discover new meanings which he perceives.

Actual freedom in evaluation and behavior does not belong to man from the first moment of conception and birth. Man must conquer his freedom. The first responses which he made to the world as a little child were usually not free, but very much conditioned by the situation in his immediate environment. In the course of his maturation, he has to transcend increasingly this unfree aspect of his life, although this does not mean that he should reject all responses to reality and to people which he adapted in childhood. It may very well be that he realizes later that many of the attitudes instilled in him as a child are quite realistic and in tune with his individual personality. In that case, becoming free means that he now ratifies such attitudes, perceptions, and orientations; from now on, he will live them by free choice as he lived them in the past by imposition. This personalization of formally impersonal habits leads to a new dimension in the actual way in which he lives these customs. They are still the same, and yet they are different. Somehow they are more alive and more solidly rooted in the core of his being. They are deeper, less mechanical and peripheral. Their insertion in the free core of his personality makes them participate in the unique, dynamic movement which he is as a whole. As a result, the freely ratified habits of a person are more flexible and more naturally in tune with the whole of the situation in which the person lives and acts. As long as an attitude or habit is not ratified by the person's freedom, it does not fit smoothly and harmoniously into the total profile of his existence. Rather, it retains somewhat the character of isolation as if it has a life of its own or as if it is a function in its own right without much relationship to the whole spontaneous mode of being of the person.

This functional characteristic of good attitudes which are not yet ratified by the freedom of the person may make his behavior somewhat disjointed and not embedded in the natural rhythmic flow of his existence. One can compare this with the art of politeness. A person may be trained in all the external ways and customs of polite behavior; he may memorize a volume on etiquette. One may even train him when to smile or to tell the right story that will be enjoyed by a host or hostess. Nevertheless, as long as this training remains at the outside as it were, and does not touch the core of his personality, it will remain artificial and without warmth. Moreover, he will not know how to adapt his behavior to changing situations not foreseen in the manuals. That is, some situations may call for behavior that is in straight contradiction to the general rules of etiquette, and, in exceptional cases, it may be most polite to be impolite. In other words, becoming free not only means that my counselee will be able freely to change behavior that is undesirable in his life, but it also means that he comes to those evaluations, attitudes, and behavior patterns which are desirable, but which up to this moment were only imposed additions to his personality. Making the impersonal become personal, rooting the unrooted, assimilating the unassimilated, ratifying the unratified, therefore, is as much an essential part of the process of discovering

freedom as the transcendence of perceptions and behavior which are incompatible with the totality of
one's personality.

My counselee has to find out how to be free. The
authentic man is not representative of freedom but
growth in freedom. The inauthentic man is not totally unfree but has stopped growing in freedom.
The outcome of good therapy and counseling is such
that my counselee will be able without me to grow
daily in freedom. My counselee comes to me because
there is something in his life that hampers his growth
in free evaluation of reality or makes it impossible to
coordinate gradually his behavior with his free evaluation. I should realize that the potential freedom of
every man can grow but, at the same time, is limited in
its actual growth at a given moment by the finite historical situation of the person concerned. I should respect the unique potential freedom of my individual
client as different from the potential freedom of myself, my friends, or of other clients whose historical
situation may be quite different. A client with low intelligence, a poor family background, and long-standing unwholesome habits of living cannot grow in freedom at the same rate and with the same intensity as a
person of high intelligence with a very secure and rich
family life, and with wholesome attitudes. As a good
counselor or therapist, I respectfully follow the pace of
my patient. And if, on the other hand, I set a pace
arbitrarily or implicitly encourage my counselee to

strive after a mode of life for which he is not yet ready, I may destroy or hamper his freedom. For what may happen is that he, not being able to live this ideal attitude from the depth of his existence, starts to imitate blindly the behavior which I impose on him by my gentle prodding; then he falls into the same trap in which he was caught already.

But the aim of therapy and counseling is precisely to free him from this trap, not to set up another one. It is infinitely better that my counselee does a good thing in an awkward and deficient way but in a free and personal fashion than to perform such behavior in splendid perfection which is merely external and the fruit of my suggestion and encouraging approval. It is a great wisdom to be satisfied with the limited freedom that each person can reach. Many people who come into counseling suffer from lack of freedom because other people pushed them beyond their limits. As a result, they are out of touch with their own depth. They are like fledgling little birds which were thrown out of their nest too early by their impatient, ambitious parents. As a result they are estranged from their own real self and alienated from their own potentialities. They play anxiously a role which is too big for them. They walk around in beautiful clothes which do not fit and are tripped up at every crossing.

This problem is also related to religious counseling. Many people who come for religious counseling have lived their religion in an inauthentic way. Having heard or read about religious perfection, they started to imitate the perfect religious attitudes in their external religious behavior. Soon there came a split between their real personal inner life and the proliferation of perfect manners, customs, and devotions which they had assumed to the great delight of their excited educators. The latter, animated by the best intentions, did not realize that they were producing a number of neurotics instead of saints. The religious counselor will soon discover, if he tries to free such patients, that it is entirely threatening to them to substitute the great and splendid virtue which is not their own for the little awkward virtue which can really spring from their deepest personality.

It may at this point be clear that counseling and psychotherapy fulfill a need which should have been fulfilled by the family, the home, and by education. For although family life and education should ideally be able to make people free, frequently the opposite happens. Instead of making the child or the pupil free, it enslaves him to the opinion of his parents, teachers, or clergymen. This does not mean, of course, that these opinions are necessarily wrong. They may be excellent. However, the crux of the matter is that such excellent ideas should be owned by the pupil himself. The teacher should be an honest witness for the good,

the true, and the beautiful. Likewise, he should create
the ideal condition in which the child himself can
awaken to these values; and the most ideal condition
for this awakening of spontaneous insight and estimation is not to force such ideals upon him. In that case
we prepare him only for hypocrisy or an uncreative
mechanized life or even neurosis.

Openness and the Willing of Reality

If counseling, then, is a making free of the person
and is an appeal to the freedom of my counselee, I
could say also that counseling directs itself primarily
to the will of the person. However, when I say that I,
as a counselor, try to awake the dormant will of my
counselee, I have to be careful not to use the term
"will" in an unwholesome sense, for the human will
has been frequently misunderstood. When I distort the
authentic nature of the human will, I distort the whole
of human life; for as we have seen, the will, the core of
freedom, is the center of human existence. My whole
conception of man is dependent on a sound appreciation of what the will is. Both counselor and counselee
may be unconsciously influenced by a mistaken notion
of the human will which is still influential in our society today. When we realize our mistaken notion of the
human will, we may respond to the discovery with an
anxious overreaction. We may be inclined to throw
the baby away with the bath water. In this case, the

abuse of the notion of free will may lead us to deny the possibility of any free will.

Why is it that we are inclined to misunderstand the human will and its function? It would seem that this misunderstanding is related to our general tendency to objectivate man's life into thinglike categories. We tend to think about man in the same manner in which we think about chemical compounds and dynamic forces and energies in nature. Thus, when we think about the will, we portray to ourselves a kind of isolated force of energy that is somewhere present in our personality like an explosive in a gun chamber. Or we imagine that the will is a kind of person in us who like an engineer controls all the buttons which make us think and move. In this conception the will becomes a kind of a thing, an absolute and autonomous power which is isolated from the whole of my personality. I become a person who, among other things, has also a curious possession called "will." This view of the human personality makes the human person like a box or a treasure-chest in which you can find a fascinating collection of all sorts of curiosities such as a fantasy, a perception, a will, or an emotionality.

This view is misleading. I do not have a will, but I *am* a will, or even better, I am a willing person. In other words, I don't find myself in the world as a person involved in daily life who has, also, somewhere a forceful peculiarity called "will," but I find myself engaged in the world at times as a willing person. Willing is thus an expression, a mode of being of myself as a whole interacting with the totality of my life situation. It is not true that my will is naturally separated from all that I am and from the world in whch I live and move and act. On the contrary, if I try to cut off my will from the whole of my lived reality, I introduce an artificial split into my life. I arbitrarily make a separation between my real life and what I imagine to be my will. I build an unnecessary and artificial opposition between two halves of me: namely, between an imagined absolute will power on the one hand and, on the other, the rest of my personality and the world that I fancy should be forced, pushed around and controlled by this will power.

In that case, we should not really speak about "willing" but about "willfulness." Webster defines willfulness as being "governed by the will, without yielding to reason; obstinate; perverse; stubborn; as a *willful* man or horse." These qualifications describe willfulness as tyrannical and unrealistic, while its performance becomes increasingly isolated from other aspects of my human existence. Why is it that willfulness is tyrannical and unrealistic? It is so because of the fact that the will is no longer a dimension of the whole personality which is willing, but elevated to a principle all of its own which does not pay any attention to reality.

As we have seen, however, man lives in an original openness for reality, or even more precisely, man *is* fundamental openness for reality. It is the very nature of my counselee to listen to reality, and this readiness to listen is already a primary way of willing. The person as willing, my counselee as willing, is first of all an openness to all manifestations of reality in himself and in his life situation. A separate "will" is simply an imagination. It is this radical openness for reality which makes man different from trees, mountains, and rivers; for the tree grows toward the sky, the mountain top pierces the clouds, and the river finds its way in the country without being aware of the surroundings, without taking any stand toward the environment; but it is the nature of my counselee to be aware of his life situation and to finally take a personal position toward the daily reality which he encounters. In other words, my counselee is in a dialogue with his environment, although his dialogue may be dormant or severely restrained because of anxiety, neurotic guilt feelings, or compulsions. I, as a counselor, must create a situation which will make it easier for my client to restore this full dialogue with the world.

To have a full, open dialogue with reality is to will reality; therefore, willing is being open to the world as it manifests itself in my daily surroundings. Conversely, the lack of willing is to close myself to the appearance of reality in my life. It is the refusal to listen to the voice of reality.

The counselor enables his counselee by his loving, therapeutic care to find the courage to will the truth— to will reality. He needs this courage very badly, for the lack of this courage made it impossible for him to face reality before the hour of counseling. Perhaps it was not his personal will that he did not dare to risk the manifestation of truth in his life. Possibly his parents were not able or willing to create an atmosphere at home in which it was easy and natural to face truth, to express the truth, or to admit the truth. Perhaps the main ambition of the family was not the realization of truth but to look good, to make a pious, talented or polite impression on the neighborhood, even at the expense of truth. Maybe it was the primary concern of the parents to feel good about themselves and about their children. Consequently, nobody was ever allowed to face and to express less attractive truths about the deficiencies, the lower needs, the base inclinations that were as much a part of this particular group of human beings as it is of all human beings. The parents did not realize that one pays a horrifying price for the suppression of the truth. Whenever one starts to close himself off from the truth, not to will truth any longer, he cuts in two the very root of human existence and human growth, for man can only grow by willing truth. All emotional disturbance is, in the last analysis, always based on an unconscious or conscious refusal to face life as it is. Therefore, instead of thinking about the will as some kind of isolated powerhouse somewhere in a personality box, it is necessary to see it as a dimension of the person as a

whole. One should realize that it is the willing openness for truth, not a kind of absolute force that in
splendid isolation pushes the rest of one's personality
around like a boxer in the ring knocks around a weak
opponent.

It may be asked how a one-sided misconception of
the human will came about. In reply, the caricature of
what human will basically is, can be explained by the
consideration of two aspects of the will. The first
aspect of myself as a willing person is openness for
truth, goodness, and beauty as manifested in my life
situation. This manifestation of reality in my life situation, however, contains an appeal to me; for as a
human being I am called not only to seek reality, but
to respond to reality. The revelation of my reality is, at
the same time, an invitation to live my existence in
accordance with this reality. The revelation of my
reality is the revelation of my life vocation. The willing openness for the manifestation of reality, the silent
voice of the situation implies the willing readiness to
bring my life gradually in tune with the truth that is
unveiled for me.

My life, its style and realization, should flow from
my perception of reality like a river flows from a
crystal clear source high in the mountains. The counselor enables the client to open up that spring and then
to let the pure water of truth find its way in the rocky,
dry, and resistant ground of daily life. A river, how-

ever, finds its way patiently in the current of many years, overcoming the resistance of stones, rocks, trees, and sand which block its way. The same is true in the life of my counselee. That is to say, he uncovers the hidden well in the depth of his being; truth reveals itself to him and now wants to incarnate itself in his daily life. The pure water of truth, however, will find in him the stone and rock of anxieties, human respect, long-standing bad habits, and laziness and inertia. Therefore, to become true as a person who wills the truth in his life, means, in the beginning, the experience of resistance. Like the river which patiently takes many years to shape its way in rocky mountains, so my counselee should, with infinite, relaxed patience, take a lifetime to realize the vision of truth that was revealed to him in the hour of therapy. As long as he shows the slightest impatience or inclination to force the issue, to push himself into the new ideal that appeals to him, he shows that he is not yet totally open to all manifestations of truth. For it is one of the most unmistakable aspects of reality that the life of man can only be changed over a long span of time. At the very moment that my counselee attempts or desires to go faster than reality allows, he is in untruth. He stands in the shadows; he moves in the wrong direction. It is then a betrayal of reality, an assault on the truth to desire or to strive to be virtuous, good, or perfect in a short time. Such an unthoughtful or proud attitude leads necessarily to an untrue, artificial life. For it will again lead to the basic problem we have mentioned before: the only achievement possible in a short time is an external semblance of virtue and perfection which is not rooted in the free, unique core of man's personality. Again, his impatience does not make him good, but makes him look good. Therefore, one of the tasks of the therapist or counselor is to spot this unwholesome impatience, this untruthful eagerness, this tense desire to realize at once the truth which has been revealed and which can only be realized partially during a whole lifetime. Here again the counselee should realize that the result of good counseling should never be any form of perfection. To be man is never to be perfect but to strive in willing openness toward a limited perfection which one is allowed to reach in one's life.

Willfulness and the Distortion of Reality

After this description it may be easier to understand where the untrue and inauthentic notion of the will as willfulness came from. Willfulness is the conceited abuse of the second aspect of willing. We speak about willfulness in a person who tries to implement too fast, too impatiently, and too forcefully a truth which is revealed to him as the truth of his life. This willfulness leads to a lessening or even a destruction of the truthful life. There is, however, even a worse possible form of this destructive willfulness. Imagine a person who

EXISTENTIAL COUNSELING

has not a willing openness to the truth, in the first
sense of willing. He, not seeing the unique truth of his
own voice, lives an alien existence and may only develop the second aspect of willing, namely, the aspect
of implementation without knowing what is the
unique truth he possesses to implement. The source of
the truth is not in himself but in books or in the description of great heroic or saintly lives of other people
or, even worse, in people around him. In this case, we
do not have a real personal dialogue of man with his
reality, but rather a blind and isolated drive to imitate
slavishly the truth of other lives.

In literature, we may sometimes find a misguided
author who describes the function of the will in this
sick and distorted way. Such authors are dangerous
because they foster neuroses in people. Here again it is
of the utmost importance for the counselor to be alert
for the slightest inclination in his counselee to make
him, the therapist, the source of the truth of his life. If
the counselee should succeed in this, the therapy
would be a complete failure, since the aim of therapy
is that the counselee finds the source of truth within
himself and not in anyone else.

As we have seen, willfulness leads to an over-
strained spastic life which makes it impossible for the
counselor to listen to the silent voice of reality in the
core of his being. This inability to listen to all the
aspects of the situation in which he lives leads to another complication. If one cannot listen to the unique

aspects of the ever-changing life situation, then he is at a loss for the right and sensitive response to the situation in which he finds himself. He becomes insensitive, unrefined, and undiplomatic in his interaction with others. All sensitive, thoughtful interaction with people and events finds its source in this relaxed openness for all aspects of the reality of these persons and situations. If one cannot be open to truth in himself and others, he has to find a substitute for the subtle voice of unique reality. It is for this reason that the person who cannot listen has to invent a compulsive code of stilted, identical reactions available for situations which he has categorized in advance. One knows exactly how he will react if he is supposed to be kind, or angry, or authoritarian, or "nice." It is as if this helpless person, out of tune with reality, anxiously asks, "What am I supposed to be in this situation? Do I have to turn on nice behavior, kind reactions, or am I supposed to be angry now?" As soon as he gets an inkling of what he is supposed to be, he willfully pushes the right button and plays his little role like the complicated old puppet clocks of the Baroque period. One can imagine what confusion such a person suffers if the same situation requires, in its reality, a subtle change of many attitudes.

The willful person has cut off all bridges with anything beyond his own willfulness. He has assumed a compulsive instead of dialectical attitude toward his existence in the world. In such a case, compulsive command replaces respected dialogue. His willfulness manipulates all other objectivated "things" in his personality and situation without respect for the subtle complexity of reality in himself and others. Soon his willfulness may tempt him to overpower, distort, and transform reality in himself and others. If he cannot listen to the subtle manifestation of rich reality in his environment, he will necessarily try to impose his willful codes on others. If a person is not open to reality and does not obey the voice of reality, a terrible distortion takes place. Sooner or later he will turn the whole relationship around: Instead of his listening to reality in people and events, he becomes convinced that reality in people and events should listen to him; instead of surrendering to the manifestations of reality, he will attempt to subject reality to himself. If the reality of people and situations speaks a language other than that which he wants, he will deny what is reality. He will call it a lot of nonsense, weak sentimentality, impractical attitudes, or lack of businesslike behavior; for all that does not conform to his code is necessarily unreal in his view. As a counselor, I may find many counselees who are excessively proud of their pragmatic, businesslike, no-nonsense attitude, or their compulsive organization and what they call their "honest expression" of all that they think.

If the therapy is successful, they will experience the fact that they must drop these attitudes which are their pride, but which cloud their view of the subtle and refined aspects of reality in their lives. Willfulness, thus, perceives reality in a categorical way. This means it does not perceive reality in its individual unique appearance, but it forces unique appearances into its prefabricated categories. Willfulness closes itself to reality as it reveals itself to the spontaneous openness of the person. Willfulness in daily behavior leads to a stilted repetition of reactions which conform to a prefabricated code. These reactions do not take into account all perceptible meanings of the life situation.

CHAPTER IV

THERAPY, WILLESSNESS AND EXISTENTIAL WILL

WE have now seen how a faulty view of the nature of the human will leads to a rigid and forced type of existence. The man who comes to me for psychotherapy may live his life in a strained and compulsive way. In spite of the fact that he does not listen to his feelings and their revelations of his situation, his emotions are still active deep within him. They are like the unseen underground streams, which silently push their way through caverns that are deeply hidden under the placid fields carpeted with grass and fragrant flowers. From time to time, however, the flow which is captivated as a giant of strength breaks wildly through the rocks, and whole fields are buried under loud and frightening rumblings. Some of my counselees who could not afford to live with complexity are astounded when the quiet pace and soft routine of their life is suddenly disturbed by the crude noises of the feelings they kept underground for so long by means of their spastic will power.

Counselors and psychotherapists who see the ravages brought on by the abuse of the will naturally grow wary of will power. They are so shocked by the turbulent lives of their patients that even the word *will* becomes a dirty word for them, associated with senseless repression, meaningless control, and lack of insight and openness. They no longer realize that the will is something far deeper and richer than this isolated, secondary aspect of willing blindly cultivated by the manipulation of their clients. Therefore, it is quite understandable that even the mentioning of human will evokes suspicion among people who spend their lives in healing the ugly and festering wounds brought about by an unwise playing with will power which is like tampering with high explosives. This reaction may lead me, as a counselor, to the opposite exaggeration. I may, for example, deny the absence of any free will in my clients. I may grieve that man is basically not free but is, rather, the captive of his past and his environment or his psychological and instinctual make-up. This one-sided view of mine may be reinforced by my sociological, psychological, and psychiatric studies.

However, the frightful consequences of abused will power, combined with the impact of the studies which show the manifold determinisms of human life, may lead me to overlook the core of freedom which makes my client, as a human being, radically different from all other human beings. If I do so, I may be inclined to consider counseling or psychotherapy simply as a process of reconditioning, or as a change of one set of determinisms by another act of determinisms which are more in tune with contemporary society. However, if I succeed in this endeavor of changing the horses which will pull the same carriage, I do not really achieve human growth in my counselee. For as we have seen, the aim of counseling is growth in freedom and responsibility.

As a counselor, I use the word *responsibility* in a very special sense: namely, I mean it as "response-ability," the ability of my client to respond in growing freedom to all the determinisms which he finds in his existence. When I, as a therapist, am caught in an overreaction against the mistaken notion of will power, I may tend to deny any responsibility in my client and therewith any possibility of wholesome, normal guilt. This denial of the presence of the experience of normal guilt is closely related to the denial of freedom.

Willessness and the Denial of Guilt

The client who misunderstands his will as blind will power instead of dialectical openness is liable to be drowned in a sea of neurotic guilt feelings which engulf and crush him. He has replaced the dictates and demands of reality in his life situation by a fixed code of numerous precepts which he blindly adopts from people, publications, and situations which may be alien to his real experience. As a result, he will not only be unable to practice such a long list of do's and don'ts because of their very length but also because of the fact that they may stand in straight opposition to his whole being. Moreover, his lack of dialogue with reality blinds him for the realistic laws of time and gradualness; therefore, he feels guilty when he cannot comply at once without delay with the commandments which he has listed for himself in airtight isolation from reality. Consequently, such a client lives under the constant pressure of faults, guilt feelings which burden him all hours of the day and sometimes deep into the night, while being unable to relieve himself from their impact because it is impossible for him to realize his unrealistic ideal of life. Here again, faced with the torture imposed on so many of my clients by neurotic guilt feelings, I may feel inclined to deny the naturalness and goodness of any kind of guilt feelings. My denial of the will leads to a denial of guilt. *Will-lessness leads to guiltlessness.* I may forget that my only chance to recreate the true human life of my client is to instill in him the presence of real will, real guilt, and real responsibility. Indeed, my counselee needs to break through his inauthentic guilt and his inauthentic use of what he calls "will power." But he has to break through them in order to find authentic will, authentic guilt, and authentic responsibility which designate a unique, individual person in open dialogue with all the aspects of his life situation. Transcending neurotic guilt and neurotic self-control, then, may be defined as lifting the veil which hides the real thing. I, the therapist, must be very astute in order to know where neurotic guilt stops and real guilt begins.

As a good counselor, I shall not deny the presence of the will, but I shall kindle the real willing or free openness of my client which is dormant or buried under his neurotic attitudes. The slightest personal assumption of a stand or a position by my client in respect to his determinisms is a sign of growth. It is most important to realize that this taking of stands should be in harmony with the realism of gradualness and slowness in change. I should also be aware that the stand taken by my counselee is primarily a position assumed in the very depth of his existence and that it may take a long time before such a change can implement itself in his behavior. Any stand, no matter how far removed from the possibility of a practical application, is still fruitful as long as it is a personal decision which is in tune with reality. My counselee, for example, may have an unwholesome mode of interaction with his fellowman which isolates him from them and leaves him desperate in a desert of utter loneliness. At the very moment that my counselee decides deep inside that he no longer wants this unhealthy attitude, he is already on the road to freedom, even when it may take many years before he will be able to implement this decision.

In the beginning of counseling, my client may be inclined to experience himself as driven by the forces of society, or by his body chemistry, instincts, and unconscious inclinations while he drifts like a helpless raft in a stormy sea. This view undermines the possibility of a vital acceptance of freedom, guilt, and responsibility. As a result, his life has lost vitality and inspiration. Living becomes for him a matter of insipid conformity to a great collectivity. He becomes a robot unable to take a personal stand in regard to his own existence and to the opinions of people around him. His denial of his freedom emasculates his existential vitality and paralyzes his potential for individual decision. He loves to search for agents in his life history which he can make responsibile for his indecision and failure. Such a client loves to hear me talk about his childhood experiences which are the cause of his difficulties. The belief in their inevitable causal impact unburdens him, at least temporarily, of anxiety and guilt feelings. Soon, however, he may use it against therapy by believing that they not only absolve him from any responsibility for the past but also for the present and the future. His belief that he may be merely a puppet moved by the strings of an unknown libido or by hidden persuaders is for him a comforting escape from responsibility and therewith from guilt and anxiety. After all, is he not lost in an ocean of stimuli like a tiny toy whose pitiful plight has been convincingly depicted by psychology?

This conviction of my client covers his refusal to recognize any responsibility for the present or the future and to admit his unwillingness to face conflict and dialogue, both of which necessarily emerge when he is willing to take a stand freely among countless possibilities. My client has to realize that his actual freedom cannot be his full possession from the first moment of conception. He has to grow to the insight that he must conquer his freedom continuously and that it is his predicament to remain forever on the verge of losing it to the deterministic forces which daily encroach upon him. Man is a tension between freedom and determinism. My counselee should become aware, in the current of his therapy, that his will can never be an absolute sovereign who passes by his bowing subjects with disdain. He will understand that his will is like a constitutional monarch who needs the diplomatic dialogue with the representatives of the unruly population if he wishes to maintain his reign.

To be sure, we should not deny that man may be almost totally determined, but this is the man who has not reached the fullness of humanness. The unfree man is almost totally defined by public opinion, social acclaim, body chemistry, or neurosis, and has diminished his ability to *respond* freely to actual and past influences which he has eternalized. He does not respond, but he reacts. If my counselee is one of these unfortunate men, he should grow to the conviction that there remains in him a possibility of taking some slight inner stand which will transmute his mere reaction into a response. Every time he does so, his responsibility will expand itself and grow in strength.

As soon as he recognizes that his will can take some stand, no matter how minute, within a possibly unchangeable physical, psychological situation, he admits the existential or dialectical quality of his will which implies that he does not deny it limitation by reality. As soon as he accepts himself as a willing person, he can take some stand in every situation including even his boundary situations of failure, neurosis, and organic affliction. At that moment he outgrows the dangerous and paralyzing fiction of willessness or absolute determinism.

We can now describe the phenomenon of willessness which we find in so many of our patients. They are first of all characterized by a kind of impersonal subservience to their own impulses or to the opinions of other people around them. At the same time, they are closed for the variety of meanings of reality. They refuse, as it were, to listen to their own spontaneous perception of reality. As a result, their behavior is not an outgrowth of a deep and personal decision. In some it is rather impulsive; in others it has more the character of an impersonal conformity to the opinions and wishes of other people.

The Dialectical Quality of the Existential Will

As we have seen, we should not understand the willing person as somebody who is pushed around by an absolute ruler called "will power." Neither should the willing person be considered the mere product of determination by his own drives, his past, or his environment. The willing person, when he is wholesome, is a constant dialogue with reality as it reveals itself in him and in his situation. My counselee should grow to the insight that his life situation is not a power which determines him totally into the deepest core of his being. On the other hand, he should not imagine that his daily situation has no influence on him whatsoever. My counselee should realize that he cannot escape his life but that he may give form to it, he may shape it or recreate it. The life situation is a challenge or an appeal which comes to meet my client in its uniqueness. It demands his personal response. It is not his making, but it will make him, while he faithfully responds to its manifestations. My client, therefore, should grow in existential willing which is, fundamentally, his openness and affirmation of all manifestations of reality. In other words, it is his fundamental readiness to face and affirm reality as it reveals itself to him in his daily situation.

To be sure, it is not easy for my counselee to listen to the manifold revelations in his daily life after being for so long blind, deaf, insensitive, and unaware. In the beginning, it is really frightening for him to allow himself to become aware of so many messages of reality in himself and in his environment which he had closed out so carefully up to this moment. He is like a small animal who has lived for years under the ground. A bulldozer comes around, digs the earth open and the poor, frightened animal finds itself at once exposed to the light of the sun, the noises of the highway, the view of the hard and crusty ground, and the many dangers in his new and open surroundings. If it would have faced this reality from the time that it was very young, it would not be so overwhelmed by it; it would have an organized pattern of response; it would know how to cope with this invasion of strange new stimuli. Now, however, it needs time, protection, and help in order to find its way safely in the wide open world.

The same is true for my client. He may panic when he is bombarded with all the new problems to which he was closed up to this moment. He had built his life as a maximum security prison. Therapy and counseling sometimes seem like a bulldozer which digs open the earth and crumbles the walls. Therefore, a great part of my counseling will provide for my client the safe environment wherein he can allow himself to become aware of the message of reality that bewilders him when he starts to open up for the first time in his life. In the beginning, he may still attempt to escape by means of clever intellectual considerations. Our logical intelligence is only a very small part of our whole being; so, when my client listens only with this small part of his existence, he will be free from most of the disturbing information which reality would give to him if he would be open with his whole being. To play it safe, my counselee may tell me, with impressive dignity, that he is a man of clear, logical reason, that he is free from any emotionality, that he is one of the strong and exceptional people who would never pay any attention to something like a mood or feeling. He may tell me with touching humility that he may indeed have made many mistakes in his life and possess many real symptoms, but at least he never failed in this respect, that he always was a man of cool logic, free from any effeminate sentimentality. He is quite shocked when I tell him, "My dear fellow, the core of your whole problem is just this forced restriction to one little area of your whole existence. You are so out of tune because you never listened to reality with all your potentialities of listening; therefore, your final information is distorted, one-sided, and artificial. You are like a man who is blind and who tries to get a picture of the world of shade and color by means of an interpretation of what he hears and feels. If this blind man would see unexpectedly, his first amazing discovery would be that the world looks quite different from what he had imagined on the basis of his one-sided information. The same is true for you. You try to understand all aspects of the world, even its emotional aspects, by means of logical reasoning. Therefore, you always miss the boat in your interaction with the people around you because your emotionality is blind and you cannot find out how they feel by means of logical syllogisms."

Of course, I as a counselor should not really tell this to him in a blunt way, but I should create a situation and atmosphere in which he can discover this for himself. He should become aware that the manifold reality in and around him manifests itself daily to him, not only in his intellect and perception, but also in his spontaneous moods, feelings, and inclinations. Each one of them has the purpose to reveal to him another aspect of his reality and of his potential response. I say *potential* because such a mood tells him how he can concentrate on certain aspects of reality and in this concentration respond to it. This does not mean that he must respond to it, that he must get involved, but only that he should be aware that he *could* get involved. Only when he is aware of all potential involvements and their desirable and undesirable consequences, can he come to a decision as to what is the best type of involvement for him here and now.

This decision will be wise, realistic, and mature to the degree that he is open to as many aspects of the situation as possible, and consequently is able to weigh them, to compare them, and to balance them. As long as my client refuses to be open to all aspects of his situation, that is, the bad ones and the good ones, his authentic and inauthentic inclinations, he cannot be sure that his final decision is the one best-suited for him. In addition, if he represses the awareness of less wholesome inclinations, he may be caught unconsciously in an involvement that is rather harmful for his healthy growth. Therefore, if we understand that the willing client is primarily openness, then we can also see that his willing does not stand in essential opposition to his moods and feelings; for moods and feelings are modes of openness and sources of information. They tell him how he finds himself in the world.

Much time in psychotherapy will thus be taken up in the exploration by the client of his many moods, perceptions, emotions, imaginations, memories, and anticipations. This will take so much time precisely because it is so frightening; therefore, my client will frequently resist his own forward movement which goads him to face more and more of what he really feels. It will also require a caring presence of the therapist to the anxious client. One of the reasons why he never dared to face his real feelings and experiences was the fact that significant people around him communicated that it was bad, dangerous, indecent, irreligious, or ungentlemanlike to express what you were feeling as a child. So, it was the deep-seated necessity to be approved by others which made my counselee from childhood repress the awareness of many of his experiences. As the disapproval of others led him to bury the awareness, so my approval and unconditional care and concern must enable him to overcome the fear that he will be rejected by people when he dares to face what he experiences.

My counselee, therefore, while explaining his experiences will, in the beginning, be on his guard. He will not only explore and express what he thinks and feels, but he will also explore me and my reactions to his expressions. He simply cannot believe that I can really accept him when he brings up such frightful things about which you are not supposed to think, let alone speak. The slightest manifestation of surprise, shock, embarrassment, or indignation on my part will set therapy back for a long time because it will reinforce his worst suspicions. He will feel reaffirmed in his conviction that it is safer to hide than to face your real feelings. It will take a long time before he can overcome this anxiety. Paradoxically, when I show great enthusiasm or exhuberant approval when my counselee in his self-exploration comes up with something which I find really important, it may harm the therapy in the same way; my approval easily brings my client back into the approval-disapproval situation which robbed him of his own evaluations. Moreover, when I am less exhuberant in my approval at other moments of self-expression by my client, he will feel that he is doing less well. Before I know it, his self-exploration is no longer a true and authentic self-exploration, an exploration not directed by himself, but by the subtle suggestion of my high or low approval. In other words, I can only foster my client as freedom, as existential willing, when I promote his self-expression and exploration by my kind, loving, and caring presence which is always the same regardless of his communications. Any other attitude may unnecessarily lengthen the period of psychotherapy, for it will seduce my client at least temporarily to leave the new frightening role of self-reliance in order to find again the safety of outside approval, in this case, by the counselor.

Near the termination of counseling, my client will grow increasingly toward wise and harmonious projects of existence. As we have seen before, the embodiments of these projects in his daily life will imply not only the right attitudes but, also, theoretical and practical plans and their functional execution. We may call this the functional aspect of the will in order to distinguish it from its more fundamental, existential aspect: the will to openness and commitment.

This fundamental aspect of the will of my client in all its concrete forms is secondary in nature and merely a derivation of his authentic existential will; it is a practical consequence of primary openness. Indeed, all forms of efficient theoretical and practical knowledge on the part of my client in the service of his functional execution of a new existential project of life *presuppose* his deeper willing openness. It is this willing openness which gradually allows my client to see both theoretically and practically what he should do in his unique life situation. Therefore, while most time in counseling originally is spent in fostering this primary openness, it is toward the end of successful therapy that my client increasingly grows toward theoretical and practical insights. He explores what he should do in a practical way in order to implement the new attitudes which he has gained. Moreover, he tries out the practical realizations of his new project of life in his daily environment. When things do not work out as well as he thought, he explores in subsequent sessions why he failed and how he should attempt to find a more efficient implementation of his new ideals. The willing openness for, and commitment to, the manifestation of reality in his life situation becomes the source and foundation of all his practical judgments, choices, and actions, and of all the theoretical and practical knowledge which is needed to achieve the realization of his new mode of being in the world.

Will, as the possibility of a free inner orientation in a determined situation, is present even in organic illness. Traditional psychology and psychiatry are pervaded by social and biological determinations. Under their influence, I may be inclined to underestimate the distinction between the spontaneous inclinations of my counselee which may be linked with his own physic-psychological disturbance and the stand which his deepest self may take when he faces, accepts, and explores his inclinations. Even if my counselee has an organic illness, I should realize that his ultimate attitudes can be molded more by what his propensities *mean* to him than by the predispositions themselves. I may see, for example, in certain epileptic patients a spontaneous inclination to suicidal depression, isolation, and feelings of inferiority. But his will, the core of his suffering existence, may transcend this inclination which he is unable to dismiss. When the decision of his will transcends the inclinations which are linked with his serious illness, then his painful situation becomes a stepping stone to greater maturity and deeper authenticity. The illness of my counselee becomes for him an appeal to live more authentically; the continuous pull of depression compels him to renew his decision against the seduction of despair. It makes it impossible for my counselee to succumb to a shallow existence which is problemless and monotonous and which is as impeccable, neat, and tranquil as a carefully arranged cemetery. My counselee in this case must choose between a degenerating existence and an heroic existence. It is difficult for him to be a *decent* mediocre man. His disturbance is his most precious challenge. Similar situations may arise in relation to clients who suffer disturbances such as invincible homosexuality or pederastic tendencies, alcoholism, and nymphomania. Every new primordial decision of such a counselee in the face of destruction reinforces and strengthens his existential stand.

When my client grows to existential willing, he will have developed a personal dialectical openness to reality as it reveals itself in his daily life situation. Secondly, he will decide for behavior which takes into account, respectfully, all perceptible meanings of his situation.

Existential Will as Primordial Decision

At various times I have stressed that my counselee should grow to primordial decision. Why do we call this primordial? This most basic decision in my client is to be either open or closed to the reality of his life situation. My client is essentially free to decide one way or the other. As a human being, however, he cannot avoid the decision as such. He is not free not to act. We call this decision primordial in the sense that it is prior to any judgment, practical decision, or motivation. It is the initial act of my client which lies at the base of all of his subsequent rationalizations, practical choices, motivations, perceptions, imaginations, memories and anticipations, and defense mechanisms. The whole life of man is built upon this primordial decision. Therefore, this primordial decision is the crucial point around which the whole counseling process develops.

I should realize that such a primordial decision is unavoidable in my counselee. Unlike animals which reach their reality and actualize themselves realistically by an instinctual type of limited openness, man is made to fulfill himself realistically on the basis of his primordial decision to be increasingly open to reality. The animal finds itself in a world of circumscribed objects which are relevant to its instinctual life. This world is given to his instincts. Man, however, chooses his world by exercising his freedom to be open or closed to whatever he encounters in his environment. He decides on his world by necessity, even though he does so freely. Finally, my client's decision to openness is unique. While every man is open or closed to reality, each has his own particular way of being open or closed. Therefore, the basic ways of being open or closed will differ from client to client. This difference is related to the uniqueness of each man's life situation which implies not only his family background, environment, and education but also his psychological and physiological assets, deficiencies, and peculiar characteristics.

The person who comes to me for psychotherapy is usually one who decided in a preconscious way under the impact of an unfavorable childhood situation not to be open for all of significant reality. In this case, it was not a free and conscious decision, but a stand imposed on him under the stress of insecurity and anxiety. It was not safe to be open for all of reality. Therefore, my counseling should provide a situation in which he feels safe and secure enough to make now, on a conscious and free level, the decision to openness. This primordial openness should be understood as a radical openness. This means literally an openness at the root of his life. We could formulate such openness as a constant readiness to be open for that which reveals itself as truly relevant to his personal calling in his unique life situation. Hence, primordial openness does not imply at all that my counselee should attempt to be actually open for as many stimuli and interests as are present in the environment. This would lead to confusion and exhaustion. It means the quiet, relaxed presence to anything whatsoever that may reveal itself as truly relevant to his unique life. I should also be aware that such openness should never be misunderstood as an aggressive type of conquering activity. It has far more the quality of waiting, listening, or relaxed recollection. It has the force of no force, the strength of flexibility, and the quiet greatness of receptivity.

CHAPTER V

THERAPY, CULTURE AND TRADITION

AS we have said, existential psychology sees the counselee basically as a relatively free being in the world. The term "world" in this expression does not mean world in the sense of unknown, uncultivated, or bare nature. "World" in existential psychology means the world as experienced, perceived, humanized, cultivated, civilized, and celebrated by man; in other words, a world of meaning which is, for the great part, communicated to us in culture and tradition. You can speak in this sense of the Eastern world, the world of the Indian, of the adult, of the child, of the adolescent, or of the primitive. When I, thus, speak about my client's being in the world, I speak about his attitude toward this world of meaning in which he is born, raised, and educated, and in which he daily participates.

Most characteristic of the cultural world of meaning is an atmosphere of thought and feeling sometimes called *zeitgeist* which could be freely translated as *the mentality of the period*.

A cultural or subcultural mentality in my client is kept alive by his heightened sensitivity to certain values. This sensitivity is communicated to him by the significant people in his environment, such as his parents or his fellow workers. A tribe of Indians, for example, may foster a mentality or an outlook on reality which has at its core a heightened sensitivity for the value of the tribe as a whole, combined with a lack of sensitivity for the unique value of each individual and for other tribes. This sensitivity and mentality leads to a specific style of perception, thought, feelings, action, worship, customs, and cultural products.

While it is true that such a cultural or subcultural world of meaning is given to my client as an inescapable part of his existence, it is also true that it is not a dead collection of frozen and stilted situations. The openness which my counselee gains in my therapy should make him realize that his cultural or subcultural world of meaning is pregnant with possibilities and appeals, which clamor to be fulfilled; that the world is a domain of action for the growing freedom, not static but dynamic, a world of becoming. The more counseling fosters a real dialogue with the cultural world of meaning, the more my counselee will be able to take a stand and direct, to a degree, this changing world.

This world of meaning given by tradition and culture on the one hand limits the freedom and the possibility of choice in my counselee. On the other hand, it appeals to his freedom, for it is a subtle, rich complex of possible tasks to be fulfilled and possible stands to be taken. "Existential willing" happens always in the dialogue between my counselee and his cultural world and implied choices of possibilities presented by his culture and tradition.

Therefore, it would be unrealistic and inauthentic for my counselee to attempt to build his life in total isolation from any form of history, culture, and tradition. History belongs to the very existence of my counselee. I cannot even imagine him without tradition and history. At home he learned how to eat and dress, how to use a chair, a dish, a spoon, how to behave and speak. He was established by all these communications in the cultural world of meaning in which his parents were living, a world which was structured without my counselee, long before he was born. His family introduced him into this common cultural world and inserted him into a cultural tradition. From that moment on he was able to behave as other people in the same culture and to encounter his fellow human beings in the many patterns of behavior and customs which he and all the others experienced as the *same* in this cultural world. Everything in this sense, every custom, word, object in the culture refers in many ways to us, even to people who do not exist any longer but who have influenced the cultural development of such things as homes, dress, furniture, language, and customs.

One generation alone would be unable to build a richly structured world of meaning without the continued sustenance and inspiration of tradition. Counseling should help the counselee in his personal, exististial dialogue with the treasures of tradition, for the truly mature man is he who does not make crucial decisions without a respectful dialogue with those who preceded him in the existential *quest* in the current of history. In this personal dialogue of my counselee with the men and women of former times and also with the customs and maxims in his family and community, his personal "existential will" awakens. Without the others and without tradition he has nothing and he is nothing. And, therefore, my counselee should realize that the world in which he lives and the way in which he converses with this world are gifts from others who went before him. Culture and tradition embody this treasure. The world in which my counselee moves is not bare nature but a world, explained, cultivated, and celebrated by former generations. It is for this reason that the world can show a human face to my counselee once he has made his peace with the world and is no longer in rebellion against tradition which he identifies with only its oppressive aspects.

My counselee should grow to the wisdom that even his existence, regardless of his maturity, training, and education, always remains to some degree dependent on tradition, for existence is fundamentally coexistence. This means that it is essentially dependent on the wisdom of other people in the past or the present. Tradition is an embodiment of this coexistential wisdom. Therefore, the will of my counselee should grow to responsible decision in existential dialogue with his tradition.

But authentic counseling also enlarges the area of insight and maturity and therewith the freedom of the counselee and the degree of his independence of tradition. No amount of therapy, however, can make a counselee totally independent of the dialogue with past and present. Being really free and mature does not mean, for my client, that he is no longer essentially dependent like other people, but only that he need not lean *exclusively* on the tradition and can form personal evaluations in *certain* situations. Free and mature existence means, above all, that my counselee becomes severely aware of the limited number of situations in which he can trust his own appraisal and of the many more numerous situations in which he is compelled by his limitations to rely on traditional or communal wisdom.

Tradition represents the wisdom of the ages as embodied in our common view of the world. My counselee will increasingly discover for himself that authentic tradition which he cannot escape is dynamic and open. He will develop an attitude which enables him to continuously enrich himself by means of the treasures of tradition. Not only that, but he will in addition feel responsible for the growth and development of these treasures themselves. He realizes that he, with others, is faced with life situations in which constantly new possibilities call for a change in attitude and style. Usually, such a change in outlook and attitude will be gradual in a client, but at times during therapy, an unexpected discovery or a sudden new insight opens up for him unsuspected and overwhelming possibilities. Such a moment in psychotherapy is a turning point and, at the same time, a crisis in the history of my client. At such a crucial impasse in his existence, my client cannot find immediately the most adequate response to the meanings which are revealed to him in his situation. He should neither reject tradition nor blindly repeat what he himself did in the past or what others did before him. He should reassume the wisdom of the past in a creative way. He should read the book of tradition in the light of appeals of new meanings which he discovers in his own life and in his situation under the influence of the therapeutic process. He may make the right or the wrong decision. The wrong decision will be followed by painful failures. But authentic counseling helps him not to be discouraged and inspires him to reopen his dialogue with culture and tradition so that the present may enlighten the past, and the past the present.

We conclude that the personal dialogue of my client with his culture and his tradition is a significant manifestation of his emergence as an existentially willing person.

Project of Existence and Culture

Our consideration of therapy, culture, and tradition leads us to the problem of the integration of the personal project of existence to be discovered by my client, and the cultural project of existence to which he is committed. The project of life in my client takes shape from infancy. It is influenced by his interaction with his parents and others who communicate to him in words, gestures, and actions, the image that people in his culture have chosen as a guideline for self-realization. My client has shaped his project of existence not in isolation but in dialogue with the project that was presented to him by his culture.

As a child; my client faced himself with the eyes of his parents, and his self-perception was formed by their perception of him. The perception of his parents was influenced in turn by a cultural or subcultural view of what a successful person should be like in his society. No man is an island, not even in the formation of his project of life. To be sure, my client, while he cannot escape his culture, is called to assimilate the value-orientation of his culture in a unique, personal way. The values of his culture should become really and solely his in the current of his development. If this were not the case up to this moment, counseling would hopefully promote an attitude in him which will enable him to assimilate personally the value-orientations of the culture or the subculture to which he has committed himself.

The existential projects of great cultures and sub-cultures are ordinarily in tune with the primary given-ness of existence. Therefore they are basically healthy, wholesome, and conducive to personal growth, since they are the fruit of revered traditions, the late bloom of life experiences of generations. The sober core of such age-old wisdom is normally in harmony with the fundamentals of human existence. This wisdom, how-ever, is incorporated into customs which change with historical situations. It is this changing embodiment in concrete styles of life which may be at odds with that which my counselee fundamentally is, for these con-crete expressions of a culture are dictated not only by the vision of generations but also by the demands of changing situations in which this vision has to be real-ized. My counselee may tend to confuse the core of the accumulated wisdom of his culture with these his-torical accretions. Such accretions are frequently the result of people's practical view of situations.

Most people are struck by immediate problems and their solution; they are not so much interested in the consideration and development of long-range attitudes and ideas. For example, how to prevent sexual dis-turbances in school or city is a question more crucial to them than the problem of what sexuality is all about. Eager to force a practical and safe solution, they prescribe and develop customs which are not chastity in itself but which, at a certain moment, are most useful to safeguard sexual values in children who are threatened by certain passing aspects of a definite situation. After some time has lapsed, people may forget about the ultimate purpose of these customs or the incidental temporary reason why they were developed. They no longer consider them to be safeguards, but they make them an end in themselves. If people are not careful, these customs may even take the place of the cultural values themselves, which they were assigned to protect. In that case, accidental customs take on a life of their own. Their life is no longer rooted in the values of religion, culture, or subculture. They loom up before my confused and frightened client as isolated powers.

A certain culture, for example, may forbid an unmarried woman to meet a man if she is not accompanied by a chaperone. Each woman may assimilate this custom in a personal way. One woman of such a culture may live it in a fashion, flexible enough to adapt itself to sudden situations not foreseen by cultural regulations. If such a woman finds herself by incidence alone with a man, she will not experience panic. Instead, she will implement the purpose of the taboo in efficient behavior. Another woman, however, may accept the same customs in a rigid manner. Instead of absorbing the ultimate purpose of the custom into her existence in a wholesome way, she makes the taboo an absolute aim in itself. Therefore, she feels guilty and upset in the same situation in which the other woman is able to relax and create new safeguards embodying the attitude and purpose expressed in the cultural custom.

The case of the two women exemplifies at least three layers of experience in the structure of a personal project of life. First of all is a personal layer, for the women live a common cultural project of behavior and attitudes in a personal way. Beneath this personal level we find another structure, an infrastructure of customs that is common to all members of a given society. The custom of being chaperoned exemplifies this infrastructure. The cultural taboo is an integral part of a system of customs that characterize this culture. We may call this second layer the "cultural customary structure." Such a cultural system of customs, however, does not drop from the sky. It develops gradually over centuries and it changes with historical situations. In spite of change in customs, however, the culture remains essentially the same and recognizable as such. The stability in this case is that there is something deeper which underlies both the cultural customs and the personalization of these customs by each member of the community. This deeper infrastructure of the culture is formed by the fundamental cultural value-orientation of which the customs are the temporary incorporation. We may call this third layer the "fundamental attitudinal infrastructure of the personal project of existence."

In the example given above, the principle of virginity prior to marriage is an aspect of this fundamental attitudinal infrastructure of a culture. The custom of chaperoning is an example of the temporary incorporation of the fundamental purpose into a safeguarding behavior which may be helpful and meaningful within a certain historical situation. The first woman cited in our example was sufficiently open to the fundamental attitudinal infrastructure of her culture to be able to create a new incorporation of safeguards of these basic attitudes at the moment that the cultural customary safeguard broke down; the second woman was not because she was so accustomed to living the safeguarding temporary custom as an absolute value in itself, and not as a passing and changeable mode of expressing and protecting the fundamental cultural value. My client should become aware that cultural and personal customs may change when concrete situations change. For example, social change brought about industrialization and may make chaperones dispensable. In such a case, the taboo may change, but not necessarily the underlying value-orientation. The deep central values which form the heart of a culture will express themselves in other taboos which are in tune with both this central value and this changed situation in which the value has to be lived. For example, women of an eastern culture who discard their veils will develop other safeguards of the marital values maintained by their culture.

My client should, thus, realize that there is tremendous room for change in his existential project on the personal level and even on the level of cultural customs, but not so on the level of his most fundamental religious and cultural attitudes so long as he wishes to remain committed to his religion or subculture. Both he and I, the counselor, should be careful not to identify this deepest foundation of his religious or cultural values with their passing expression in contemporary customs and in my client's contemporary life. To be sure, I may discover that my patient lives with principles of his religion and culture in an unwholesome and anxious way. But, if I identify this unhealthy expression with the principles themselves, I may unconsciously communicate to my client that I cannot appreciate his principles as something of potential value for his personal existence. In this case, I may unwittingly drain the motivating power from my patient's fundamental cultural project of existence with which he might eventually have a fruitful healing dialogue.

Suppose, for example, that my client is an Amish woman whose marriage is unhappy because of her neurotic frigidity. I realize during the treatment that she feels that sex is something despicable. She tells me about the rules of dating behavior in her Amish community, customs which were designed to safeguard in the young the principles in the Amish culture relating to sexual relationship. My further exploration confirms my suspicion that these rules of dating were interpreted by my client to mean that sexuality itself is bad and distasteful. In the course of therapy, however, she becomes aware that her conclusion is unjustifiable, that other Amish women subject to the same customs are not frigid, that there must be something wrong in the way in which she has understood the customs of her people. This growing awareness helps her to see sexuality in a different light, without rejecting the cultural-religious ground of her existence. If I should prematurely identify my client's unwholesome attitudes with Amish sexual principles, however, I should be in danger of hindering her recovery.

After dealing with many similar cases in a particular population, I may become suspicious about certain aspects, not of their fundamental attitudes, but of the customs in which they incorporate these attitudes. I may suspect, for example, that they have a manner of communicating the safeguards of sexuality which leads to neurotic anxiety in sensitive young people. At this point, I may be tempted to overstep my area of competence; I may be rash enough to suggest new customs for a subculture alien to me. But it is not my task as a psychotherapist to attempt to change the sexual safeguards of the various populations in my pluralistic society. Only the unique subculture or religion itself can create new safeguards which do not betray its fundamental project. To be sure, I may respectfully suggest that a re-evaluation of safeguards might be desirable. I may intimate, for example, that the leaders of the subculture might profitably alter the language in which the several customs are communicated, since only those who live this in culture can do so in a manner which will leave its foundations intact. Only the leading thinkers of a religion or culture are capable of returning to the source from which their religion or culture originated. This return to the source enables them to distinguish between what is fundamental and what is incidental in their customs and safeguards. We may call this procedure "re-sourcing." When the psychotherapist puts up the danger sign, it may be time for a religion or subculture not to deny its heritage but to return to its sources.

As a psychotherapist, I may make another mistake. I, too, am rooted in a subculture which may differ from that in which my patient has anchored his life. If I am not careful, I may unconsciously impose on my client my own view of existence. An unguarded reaction, a slight impatience may communicate better than words to my counselee what I really feel. I may unwillingly suggest to him that he should integrate his project of life within the cultural structure of my own project of existence. If he attempts to do so, of course, he will fail, because my project of life is rooted in a cultural ground which my client does not share with me. The religious or cultural project which I live may be for my client a mere outline without roots in his own tradition. The imposition of my cultural view may result in a new split in my patient's attitudes; for in the depth of his existence he is rooted in his own religious or cultural project, yet he develops an alien project of life which I have unconsciously communicated to him. His life will, in such a case, be regulated from two conflicting centers: the project of his own culture, and that of mine, his psychotherapist. I could have prevented this conflict if I had been aware of the impact of my own world-view on my therapeutic communicaiton, if I had really understood the background of my patient's life, or if I had distinguished between his religious or cultural infrastructure and the neurotic manner in which he attempted to implement the structure.

I should, thus, be aware that my own style of life has been formed in the light of my experience and those people in my surroundings. The cultural component of my style of behavior and perception developed in the light of the image of "ideal" behavior that was held by the people of my home, neighborhood, and society. The style of life which I believe to be ideal permeates my human relationships and is particularly evident in the meetings between me, as a counselor, and the counselee who presents himself to me with his problems. From our discussion, it may be clear by now that the secret influence of this idealized norm may be harmful. Existence as embodiment in space and time necessitates that I am present to others in some style of life. However, my personal embodiment of existence is not the only possible or desirable one for everybody else. The unconscious identification of my personal way of life with "the" way may limit my therapeutic relevance to that part of the population which is spontaneously in touch with my style of being, while it averts others or perverts them to an attempt to be what they are basically not.

Therefore, as a counselor, I should grow daily in the awareness of my prereflective attitude. Of course, I cannot do away with my personal style of existence; as a human being, I must embody my mode of being in concrete behavior, which is always limited in space and time and, therefore, necessarily one-sided. But I can increasingly free myself from the identification of existence as such with my personal-cultural style of being. This inner freedom will enable me to sense the unique potentialities in those counselees who differ from me in expression and preception. When I am deeply aware that my own pecularities are incidental and transient, I will distinguish what is essential from what is accidental. This self-awareness will enable me to transcend the temporal, to become aware of my cultural and subcultural stereotypes, of my antipathies and sympathies; my emotional blocks will become manifest to me in this maturity. I may discover, for instance, that I a priori do not like people with aesthetic inclinations because the good farmers at home confused artistry with frivolity. Or I may realize that I onesidedly prefer "regular guys" because as a high school or college student I disliked some pale companions who were delighted more by books than by baseball. Another counselor may find that he is unconsciously enamored with scholarly types because he is fed up with his more pragmatic colleagues who make fun of him. Or a counselor may discover during this process of growing up that he unconsciously favors a certain compulsiveness because he has identified the compulsive mode of being with sound strictness and, consequently, distrusts spontaneity in himself and others.

We conclude, then, that it is of the utmost importance that I, as a counselor, do not suggest to my client in any way that he should accept my personal mode of being or my cultural project of existence. To be sure, a fruitful cultural project of life should not be at odds with the fundamental structure of existence itself. If it is, it is unwholesome. It is unnatural and, therefore, disruptive. But the great religious and cultural traditions which developed over many centuries are at least basically compatible with the fundamental structure of man's nature. This does not mean that such a culture or religious project does not orient and limit the inexhaustible possibilities of living a human life for my counselee. It is precisely the essence of wholesome tradition to present man with a frame of value-orientation which respects his natural creativity, gives room for his unique personal development, and at the same time shapes his life in certain directions and not in others.

A Tibetan from the Himalayas differs in cultural tradition and orientation from a New Yorker. Nevertheless, the life of both can be consonant with the basic nature of man, and each can freely personalize his own cultural frame in one of an inexhaustible number of individual projects of life. In each case, the religious, cultural, or subcultural frame of values and insights gathers to itself the existential wisdom of the past and proposes a style of existence that has served countless others in an integrative and not in a disruptive way. As long as my counselee honestly means to commit himself wholeheartedly to such a religious or cultural tradition, he should be loyal to its basic tenets, if not to all its changing customs. Otherwise my client will suffer a split in his existence. He has either to change his commitment or integrate his life within the fundamental frame of his commitment. This decision is his own. I, as a psychotherapist, should not make it for him or even suggest it to him.

As a psychotherapist in a pluralistic society, in short, I should understand and respect the various subcultures of my patients. I should learn to distinguish between the value-orientations of these subcultures and the changing expressions of these values in passing customs and safeguards. I should also be aware of the variety of ways in which individuals may realize these values, customs, and safeguards in their unique personalities. I can grow in the wisdom requisite for such insight only to the degree that I am able to transcend the defenses and attitudes which my own environment may have instilled in me concerning cultures, subcultures, and religions which differ from my own.

The methods of training psychologists, psychotherapists, counselors, and social workers are legion. Do they all take into account the fact that these therapists are being trained for a pluralistic society? How many seminars are dedicated to the understanding of the varied cultural, subcultural, and religious projects of existence which underlie the lives of their patients? Is there a sufficient number of group therapeutic sessions in which the students can work through their own unconscious hostilities and defensive misunderstandings of religions or cultures which are not their own? Is it still possible for a person to qualify as a therapist in our pluralistic society even though he has not yet developed a sympathetic understanding of its main religions and subcultures? Such courses for therapists should communicate not the highly developed theological or philosophical elaborations of these religions and subcultures but rather their existential structure: what existence really means to these people; what it really feels like to them.

Integration of Personality and Culture

The therapist or counselor must help the client to become aware of how he lives his daily life in relation to his own project of existence. My client has to realize the discipline which his own project of existence imposes on his daily life. If my counselee freely acts against his own commitments, he cannot live with consistency and unity. His life will remain disintegrated and consequently disruptive. My client must therefore clarify for himself how he concretely lives his existential discipline; how he embodies it in behavior and perception.

We may clarify the problem of integration in my counselee by an analogy. The integration of a particular into a larger unity always implies a restriction of both the particular and the whole which assimilates it as a part. When I build a house, I impose restrictions on the specific materials which I use. The bricks I use in my walls cannot be used for my fireplace. On the other hand, the fact that I use bricks imposes restrictions on my house. I must adapt the foundation and the structure of my house to the proportions of stone. If I had used wood instead of brick, the structure would have been quite different. Again, when there is a fault in the construction of my house, when walls begin to crumble or bricks begin to tumble down, I may consult an expert in architecture or engineering. I shall expect him, at least, to respect my original project and not to advise me to rebuild my house in wood instead of brick. The only thing I shall ask him is *how* to reintegrate the bricks within walls which are designed to sustain the type of home I have chosen to live in.

To be sure, a man is not a home, a project of existence is not a blueprint, and the dilapidation of a building differs from the disintegration of a life. Nevertheless, there is an analogy between material integration and the various dimensions of human life. There is a likeness, too, between the behavior of an expert who is called in to restore a disintegrating building and that of the counselor who is called to assist his client in his reintegration of a split existence.

Discipline is essential for integration. The fact cannot be changed, for the necessity of discipline is rooted in the very structure of human existence. But the concrete ways in which my counselee lives his discipline are open to change and development. Sound discipline presupposes that my client becomes aware of all his modes of existence and his real appreciation of each one of them. A depreciation of any mode of being leads to repression and isolation. A repressed mode of being cannot be integrated with my client's total existence. On the other hand, the client who over-values, in an isolated way, one mode of existence without relation to the others faces the same problem of disintegration as the one who depreciates and undervalues it. For example, a patient who lifts nudity as an isolated ideal from the whole of existence no longer knows how to integrate the mode of being nude into the total mode of being a man.

In short, a patient should discover that the integration of existence presupposes a wholesome project of life, a sound appreciation of all his modes of existence, and a readiness to discipline his modes of existence in the light of the project to which he has committed himself. I say "readiness" for it is clear that willingness does not always succeed. Failure is unavoidable, especially in the neurotic patient. An existential project is precisely a project; it is not a summary of what I have already achieved, but a design of what I hope to realize more and more. As long as my counselee honestly attempts to live a wholesome project, he should not be crushed by guilt because of his repeated failures. He should learn that his project is his compass, not an assurance of success. It helps him to know where he is going, even when the going is rough.

The integration of existence is a life-long task for the counselee. As a human being, he can grow in countless possible directions. However, he cannot grow in all directions at the same time. This would be chaos. His existence would be meaningless, a tale told by an idiot. Therefore, some project of life is necessary if my client's development is to have meaning. Inner propensities and social pressures during his childhood formed the hesitant beginning of his project of life. We have seen that a sound project of existence is in tune with the fundamental structure of human nature. This structure implies that man lives in a world of meaning, that many possibilities of fulfillment are offered to him in everyday life. On the other hand, the same human structure reveals to me that my counselee is basically free, that he himself can decide in what manner and to what degree he will respond to these invitations. If my counselee desires to integrate his existence in a whole-some way, his personal answer to the manifold appeals of the world will be compatible with his project of life.

My client's project of existence, if it is wholesome, will not contradict his fundamental nature. In sharing a project of life in harmony with existence, however, my client is not alone. No man is an island. Existence is coexistence. This fact implies that countless men before my client have searched for a grand design of wholesome living, a design that would integrate a variety of modes of existence without denying the basic structure of human life. The fruit of this search of generations of men has been incorporated into the great cultural and subcultural projects of existence. No counselee can search for a project of life in a manner which implies that no one before him has ever sought for such integration or paid any attention to this matter. He cannot escape the life projects of those who have gone before him; for only man has a childhood. Childhood is an ontological structure of man; it is of the very essence of man, and no other species than he is rooted by his parents or substitute parents in some design for living during a prolonged period of helplessness and dependency. To be sure, he can later react against this pattern. But even this reaction will be colored both by the design against which he reacts and by other designs developed by other subcultures which he finds is his society. My counselee can never escape cultural influences.

Another essential structure of my patient is his relatively short lifespan. This is true of all men, seldom encompassing one century and up to now seeming never to have reached two centuries. It is therefore impossible for one individual, such as my client, to try out experientially all possible projects of existential integration in order to choose the most effective one. The only way open to my counselee is to make one of the already existing projects his own and to live it in a personal way. The available projects of existence are fundamental value-orientations and customs and safeguards within which the central orientations are incorporated. As we have seen, the fundamental value-orientation of a cultural project cannot be changed without changing the project itself. But the customs and safeguards, cultural and personal, which incorporate these fundamental value-orientations can be changed, insofar as they are superfluous to the original attitudes. Therefore, my counselee can integrate his existence in a wholesome way only if he commits himself to at least the basic value-orientation of some cultural project of existence that is in harmony with human nature and only if he makes this commitment personal and lives it in a unique creative way, since every cultural project leaves room for creativity. It is like a harbor from which to venture out into the open sea.

The integration of existence is subtle and complex; its dependence on a cultural project means a dependence on human encounters from infancy on. Such encounters were fraught with disturbance and confusion for my client. And it is for this reason that he lost his way. My counseling may help him to know where he is going, but once he knows this and has regained trust, it is up to him to make his own decisions.

CHAPTER VI

THERAPEUTIC ATTITUDES

FROM all that we have said, it is clear that the relationship between me and my counselee is the principle means for bringing to expression the world of meaning in which he lives. The quality of our relationship will determine to what degree his personal world will find expression. The first task is, therefore, to establish a relationship which fosters optimal communication. My counselee has learned to hide this personal world in order to protect himself from being misunderstood, humiliated, or abused. To reveal his personal world to me is, in a sense, to surrender his very being and to expose his sensitivity, his project of life, and to unveil his vulnerability when certain meanings which he cherishes may be at odds with the values which he supposes to be mine. This fear of disapproval limits his free admission not only of base inclinations but even of sublime aspirations. It may be very difficult for him to verbalize in my presence his finer sentiments. He may fear that the communication of refined feeling would sound ridiculous in my world of meaning. He may be accustomed to repressing these feelings because he feels that they do not have a place in the world of functional meaning which he shares with contemporary man. This repression of his personal world under the pressure of a shared social world may be so intense that my client himself is unaware of the deepest meanings which constitute his personal life. I may make myself mistakenly the ally of this social everyday world by lightly joking about noble sentiments in order to assure him that counselors are regular fellows. If I do so, I can be sure that my counselee's personal world of experience will remain a closed domain. Some counselors may cherish the illusion that such "open-mindedness" breaks barriers, forgetting that an exclusive open-mindedness for the cultural-social scene may mean a closed-mindedness for the personal world of the individual in its most revealing features.

My counselee may be tempted to identify me with his parents, teachers, administrators, supervisors, or school friends. These identifications may harm the effectiveness of my counseling, for such close relationships usually imply a withholding of the personal world so that one may function smoothly within the frame of daily life. Sometimes it may be even more advantageous when I am unknown to the client and different from the people in authority whom he meets in school, family, and society. Then, my function seems vague and unusual, as if I come from a strange, far away country. But if I am identified, on the contrary, with the authorities in the environment of my counselee, his daily mode of existence toward those people might be easily adopted toward me. Counseling would easily structure itself in terms of this mode of existence; the formal, casual, dependent, or superficially friendly features which characterize daily interactions would determine this new relationship and keep it on a level which may generate pleasantries, polite condition, or formal respect, but no experience in depth. However, when my client cannot experience me as he does his daily associates, then no stereotyped mode of existence toward me is available. He faces this ambiguous situation alone and not in the company of his friends, his fellow workers, colleagues, or classmates. Such a situation is conducive to responses which will reveal my client's unique way of being in the world and which are less contaminated by socially shared modes of existence.

On the other hand, if the ambiguity is too much to bear, it will evoke too much anxiety in my client and paralyze communication. I should, therefore, not make myself known to my counselee by being too friendly and jovial and by removing all social distance. For in that case, I and my client will act out superficial, social roles which usually prevent communication on a deeper and more personal level. Neither should I be so distant and withdrawn that my counselee freezes in anxiety. I should not maneuver myself into a situation in which I will be forced to do most of the talking; yet, I must avoid sitting there like a sphinx which would prevent the possibility of spontaneity in his communication. Such an attitude of professional composure and would-be serenity may be inspired by an unauthentic image of the "wise," "mature" man without emotion, which is a neurotic imitation of real wisdom and maturity.

Ideally, I should be experienced by my counselee as a deeply interested, wise friend whose main wish is to help him find himself in relation to his possible project of existence. However, I may be the victim of my own unconscious needs which make it difficult for me to establish such an interested, and at the same time, detached relationship. Therefore, I should examine my motives after every session. Do I need to sound like an oracle; am I in love with my own sonorous voice or clever interpretations; do I feel that I "know" people already through and through; am I authoritarian in subtle ways; do I need to be popular, to be liked or elated as a "nice chap" by my counselee; am I afraid of depth in myself and others; do I repress my own feelings and paralyze my spontaneity; or am I afraid to verbalize or to hear the verbalization of certain experiences? This list could be expanded indefinitely. It is only after a period of growth and experience that I will be able to approximate the ideal attitude which makes the relationship itself my most efficient instrument. A mature and experienced counselor is indeed a precious gift for a community.

The relationship itself which I establish as a counselor differs from the structure of other relationships. First, it is different because of its objectives, which we have discussed earlier, and second, it is different from other relationships because of specific attitudes of me, the counselor.

My attitudes aim at the expression of the personal world of the counselee. At the base of these attitudes is the genuine, unconditional acceptance of my client regardless of what world of meaning he will reveal. Any trace of disapproval diminishes the ability of my counselee to unveil his life. The full expression of his personal world can also be arrested by too great a personal involvement of mine in only one or another aspect mentioned by him. Such emotional concentration on only one aspect prevents his narration of other dimensions of his world of meaning which may be just as important for an overall understanding. I must express spontaneously all vague and confused feelings, attitudes, and motives which he may have in regard to his project of life.

I should be emotionally involved only to the extent that it is necessary to help my counselee become alive to the exploration of his world. But, my interest should be tempered and distanced to such an extent that I am able to accept all aspects of experience expressed by my counselee without reacting to them favorably or unfavorably. Either reaction may encourage a positive or negative concentration on some particular aspect of the counselee's world at the expense of the revelation of other ones. I must be a participant in the world of my client while being at the same time its respectful observer.

Flexibility

As a counselor, I should be flexible. My counseling should not be relegated to a rigid observation of rules which I have learned from books or formed for myself on the basis of experience with former clients. On the contrary, I should be convinced that every counselee and every world of meaning is in some way unique. Everything that I say and do should be the creative outgrowth of my respectful participation in this unique existence here and now. This presupposes that I am a mature person free from threat and, therefore, free from rigidity. Rigid behavior is a defense against the possible challenge of an unexpected world, when I feel unable to risk the full revelation of another world of meaning. There are two main forms of rigidity: the one leading to a stiff formal attitude in order to escape communication in depth; the other leading to a compulsively "jolly good fellow" attitude which may be an even more effective defense against a true human encounter. Sometimes we find a curious combination of both defenses in the same insecure, anxious person: in the fulfillment of functional, administrative obligations, he may be formal and rigid; while in his social relations, compulsively joking and funny. The mature person can be serious, gay, or detached according to the challenge of the situation. He adopts none of these attitudes compulsively; his behavior is not identical in different situations. My creativity as a counselor implies flexibility of attitude, feeling, and behavior in authentic response to the real situation.

Acceptance

Another fundamental attitude in my relationship with the counselee is acceptance, an attitude which generates in my counselee an experience of really feeling understood in his uniqueness and in his personal world. My counselee gradually becomes convinced that he truly shares this personal world with me. This feeling enables him to explore this world further and to communicate the outcome of these explorations with less embarrassment. When my counselee perceives that I coexperience what things mean to him and that I still accept him, he moves into a safe, experiential communion with me.

That I coexperience what people and things mean to my client does not mean that I agree with his perhaps one-sided viewpoint or that I approve of the fact that he concentrates onesidedly on this particular isolated aspect of reality. Acceptance of a person does not imply my personal agreement with his strivings and decisions as such. My coexperience and acceptance implies only a nonjudgmental attitude. Rather my whole attitude communicates to the person: I do not judge at this moment whether or not your feelings and attitudes prove that you are personally guilty for developing them; I leave that to your own conscience. My special function as a therapist is not to judge how far you are personally responsible for these attitudes and feelings, but to understand what region of your existence they reveal. Basically, I respect and like you, because deep down your nature is a gift of being; this gift is fundamentally good and, therefore, lovable, no matter how it may be overgrown and veiled by attitudes and feelings with which I do not personally agree.

The attitude of acceptance is so fundamental for effective counseling and, at the same time, so different from our usual mode of encounter that it may be fruitful to go somewhat deeper into this matter. I can accept the views, feelings, and behavior of my counselee under various aspects. For example, I might consider them as isolated abstract norms of human conduct, in which case I can accept or reject them as such. When my client mentions, for instance, that he honestly thinks that certain races should be exterminated, I cannot accept this personally and wholeheartedly as a highly commendable norm of human behavior. Or, I might consider these views, feelings, and behavior under the aspect of their usefulness for my counselee himself. For instance, I may personally dislike poetry and would not want to cultivate this interest in my own life; I may sense, however, that the poetical mode of existence may be very important for this specific client and therefore accept it under this aspect. By the same token, I would reject under this aspect a suicidal interest of my counselee. However, I do not openly express the acceptance or rejection of his judgments as isolated judgments. Regardless of my acceptance or rejection of these particular views, feelings, or behavior as isolated, absolute expressions, I always meet, accept, and respect my client himself as a worth-while human person, dynamically present in and beyond those communications. For the same attitudes are not only categories of socially acceptable or rejectable behavior; they are also manifestations of a fellow human being. They manifest that my client is not an animal, an inanimate being, or a case history; their specific content reveals that this human being has adopted certain modes of existence in the world. As a counselor, I experience primarily in all these views and behavior patterns a suffering, sometimes victorious, sometimes defeated human being who is trying desperately to come to terms with life and society. It is in this last way that I experience and accept the views and findings of my client; namely, under the aspect of their being manifestations of a struggling human person, searching for a meaningful project of life.

It is this kind of acceptance and genuine interest which opens up my client and helps him become actively involved in the process of self-discovery and its expression. A climate is created in which the flow of communication is not halted by the anxious expectation of disapproval, rejection, criticism, or any other negative responses which he might have previously experienced in family, church, school, or society at large. By creating this acceptable climate, I will also experience that my attitude mellows his defenses and lessens his resistance and his inclination to rationalize, deny, or distort hidden attitudes in order to prevent my disapproval or rejection of his personality. For there is perhaps nothing else that he fears so much as my depreciation and secret blame. On the other hand, if I am able to accept him wholeheartedly, my accepting attitude will be reinforced and deepened by a more genuine and spontaneous response from him than was possible when I was not ready to grant him unconditional trust.

I may experience difficulty in maintaining this acceptance at certain moments of interaction with my client. In that case, I should ask myself what it is in his communication to me that halts the free flow of my spontaneous acceptance. I may be surprised to find out that at times it is almost impossible to realize exactly what affects my ability of acceptance so deeply. It may well be that the counselee reveals something to me about his own life that is related to some aspect of my personality which I could never accept in myself and which I therefore have deeply buried in my unconsciousness. The same anxiety which made me bury this region of my existence in the first place closes me off again when I sense the slightest indication of the same threatening reality in another.

Imagine, for example, that I experienced at a certain time in my life the suspicion that homosexual tendencies were not totally absent in me. At that moment, I may have experienced overwhelming feelings of fear, shame, guilt, disgust, or even nausea. Threatened and tortured by these feelings, panicky and distraught, I refused to face this reality of my life; only by denying its presence did I feel able to transcend my pained consciousness. From that moment, I unconsciously developed the defense attitude which makes me close up automatically when anything threatens to re-awaken this part of me which I can not accept or face.

Envisage now a situation in which my client begins hesitantly to mention that he dimly suspects there is some inclination to homosexuality in his life. Ideally, as a good counselor, I should spontaneously and wholeheartedly accept my client as a fellow human being facing squarely this threatening possibility. My relaxed understanding and deeply interested acceptance of him as a person who is trying to come to terms with his homoerotic orientation will enable him to accept and to face this reality; otherwise, by repressing his awareness of it, he may make it a potentially explosive issue. However, it will be impossible for me to offer such spontaneous acceptance if I am unable and unwilling to face this issue in my own existence. Until I have worked out this specific problem personally or in psychotherapy, I will unconsciously sustain the defensiveness of my counselee with my own defenses. I will somehow communicate to him in my very behavior that this issue is interesting, but really not too important, nothing to be worried about, we all have these feelings at some time. Discouraged by this belittling reaction, the client gradually drops the issue. Now both counselor and client feel somewhat tense. Therapy does not flow as easily as it did before; the movement toward enlightenment has been stilted. The implicit communication of my own anxiety, in other words, has prevented the frank exploration of this specific area of life. For this reason I must continuously and thoroughly investigate and evaluate myself.

Every session with my client should be a source of relaxed self-reflection. What did I say? How did I respond? What did I feel? How did his communication affect me? Was I uneasy, excited, threatened, or at ease, comfortable, and relaxed? Why was I so? My personal existence is my main tool in counseling and psychotherapy. In order to keep myself refined and sensitive in relaxed openness for my client, I should be willing to work through my inhibitions, anxieties, and insecurities with a therapist whom I trust. I must continually refine this instrument that I myself am, for no amount of reading, study, or lectures can replace the crucial impact of my own being upon my counselee.

Gentleness

As a good counselor, I should maintain a mildness in my approach which does not interfere with the courageous facing of reality in both myself and my counselee. My mildness should not be anything sentimental, effeminate, soft, or sticky. Perhaps the word which best expresses this fundamental attitude is gentleness. Gentleness is a basic orientation of my being which reveals itself in respectful, sensitive, considerate, and tolerant modes of existence. This fundamental stand should become so much a part of me that I manifest amenity spontaneously in all situations and especially in my therapeutic encounter. It is difficult for the counselee to express himself fully if this atmosphere of gentle consideration and respect is absent. For some counselors it may seem almost repulsive to be gentle. Sometimes a male high school counselor may believe that he should convince the boys that he's just another guy who happens to be taller, heavier, and more muscular. This "regular guy" attitude may have emerged in his past when it was deeply rewarded by the approval and applause of his friends in college or high school. It may take time to realize that this same adolescent behavior will be ineffective in his new adult role where he must go beyond the peripheral and reach the core of human existence.

Another counselor may not have worked through his anxious concern about being a real man, and this unconscious preoccupation may paralyze his gentility. Others, again, have not come to terms with the loneliness of existence and are unconsciously searching for a tenderness which will fulfill their sentimental needs. Their gentility lacks spine, strength, and respect; it has a sticky quality which may repel people.

Some counselors may be masterful in their ready manifestation of an inauthentic friendliness which does not originate in the depth of their existence but is calculated and carefully added to their daily behavior in those situations in which the good counselor is supposed to be pleasant. This instant pleasantness whipped up at will like frosting on the counseling cake is practiced as a tour de force, a feat of strength, a stunt of psychological know-how and clinical cleverness. Such a forced make-believe gentility remains superficial and will not open the deeper layers of existence.

Sincerity

Finally, I should develop sincerity in the depth of my being; my attitude should be straightforward, honest, and truthful. I should be aware that I may have been compelled in my daily life to develop a social facade, a mask, a certain distance in order to protect myself against obliteration by the demands of the crowd. Everyone around me may realize that I am a good counselor and may conveniently forget that it is impossible for me to become involved in everyone's problems and at the same time to survive as a sane human being. I may have been obliged to develop a smooth, easy way of dealing with large numbers of eager beavers who accost me everywhere with their questions, neuroses, and venerations. Also, the population at large demands that I, the counselor, be "nice" regardless of my mood, my toothache, the battle with my wife, or the troubles with my principal. I realize, moreover, that the effective functioning and the minimal serenity of the school community to which I belong demands a smooth interaction between administration, faculty, and counselors. This implies certain social niceties which should be maintained on the surface no matter how I feel inwardly.

In the course of the years, I may have developed a keen facility in this external behavior which keeps the bad world of nosey administrators and wise faculty members at bay. How tempting it may be for me to fall back on these self-protecting habits when meeting a counselee who manages to threaten me as some of these people do in my daily life. However, such behavior, no matter how useful in my interactions with the community at large, will paralyze true communication with my counselees.

Counseling and Theories of Personality

I realize now that I should daily grow in openness for my client and his world and that I should develop attitudes which facilitate my optimal communication with him. The question that comes naturally now to my mind is whether the development of this openness and the related attitudes is a sufficient preparation for my counseling. I realize after all that there exists a very extensive literature on the human personality, the laws of its growth, its crises, and deviations, and the many ways in which one can analyze the life of people and the many methods one may use to help them to find their way back to reality and to themselves and their fellowmen. Should I know all these theories and all relevant scientific studies? And if I know them how should I apply this knowledge to my counseling? Should I study all theories of personality, or should I concentrate on only a few or perhaps only one? In regard to methods of psychiatry, counseling and psychotherapy, should I be trained in one or all of these approaches to the client? Is it necessary for a counselor to be an expert in psychopathology and in the extensive learned nomenclature that goes with it? Is psychological theory superfluous for counseling? If not, what is its role?

We speak here about therapeutic counseling, not about specialized vocational or religious counseling. In the latter case, it is immediately evident that we need a wide knowledge of the special area concerned. To help the counselee live his life in this specific area efficiently and harmoniously presupposes years of study and research on our part that should continue as long as we are active in this area of vocational or religious guidance. Our counselees are faced with a continuous change in these dimensions of human life and culture, and we must keep abreast of them.

Here, however, I am concerned with therapeutic counseling that does not aim at the insertion of the person in a concrete field of human life already elaborated by a complex society, but in the restoration of my client to a basic trust in himself and his world. This restoration of trust is so essential and so primordial that it precedes the possibility of any concrete introduction of the person into the fabric of modern life and its manifold functions. When I am engaged in therapeutic counseling, I encounter my client on a most primordial, simple, and direct level; that level is presupposed by the socially more complex levels on which he lives his concrete vocational, functional, and religious life within his specific denomination, if he adheres to one. From this it follows immediately that primordial encounter is far less bound to scientific information than any counseling that focuses on the more complex levels of existence. To be sure, my client, while working through his most fundamental modes of human encounter, may refer to complex social situations where his basic presence to man and reality is concretely realized, revealed, and illustrated. In therapeutic counseling, my client and I may deal with his presence on these levels. We focus, however, not on the concrete details of his effective performance as such but on what it reveals about his deepest approach to life as manifested in these practical daily endeavors.

In other words, therapeutic counseling concerns itself with primordial, vital stands in life which, in the counseling situation, have to be lived through and only secondarily thought through. This is another way of saying that I should be careful lest my preoccupation with science and theory turns my counseling session into a classroom situation instead of an authentic life situation. Let us go somewhat deeper into this issue.

The Avoidance of a Premature Use of Theoretical Concepts

As a counselor, I try to foster a self-understanding in my counselee which is free from influences which are subjectivistic. "Subjectivistic" obviously does not have the same meaning as "subjective." As a counselor, I am naturally deeply interested in the real structures and meanings of the subjective experience of my counselee. The term subjectivistic does not refer here to the real experience of my counselee, but to the explanation which he has made up himself or together with others in daily life in order to account for his experiences in terms which distort their real message.

For example, my client is a peeping Tom. If he would really be open to the structure and meaning of his experience, he would realize that he has strong sexual desires which he is unable to fulfill in his marital life because of his insecurity in regard to his adult marriage partner. This insecurity leads him to look for sexual satisfaction in immature unrealistic ways which may get him into serious trouble with the law and which prevent him from growing up to a satisfactory mature sexual relationship with his wife. An honest probing by my client in this area may reveal other larger structures of experience of which the just mentioned structure is only a substructure which embodies an over-all orientation or intentionality of my client. He may discover, for example, that he is avoiding mature encounters with his peers not only in the sexual dimension of his existence but in all dimensions, and that this orientation of his experiential life is linked to a traumatic experience in childhood. Frequently, however, my client will have a subjectivistic interpretation of his peeping behavior that alienates him from the true meaning of his experience.

For example, he may tell me, and what is worse believe, that he is not peeping at all but seriously engaged in the psychological study of the intimate life of people which he imagines he approaches with a detatched, scientific interest. I call such an explanation subjectivistic because it is not true and objectively rendering explicit what his subjective experience truly is. Instead he confronts me with an explanation that has been made up in a purely subjectivistic way. It will be impossible to discover the real objective structure of subjective experience as long as he is not able to break through this subjectivism. A great part of our naive knowledge of ourselves is made up of such subjectivistic explanations. Therapeutic counseling therefore means a purification of this naive self-understanding by a search together for the real self-experience which hides behind this curtain of subjectivistic explanations that are typical of our everyday awareness.

As a counselor, I am thus faced with the naive experiences of daily life which inhibit the access to the real experience of the person. I may try to break through this veil by bringing to the counseling situation theoretical categories which I learned in my study of psychology and which give explanation to the experience of my client other than his naive everyday interpretation of his behavior. I tell him kindly that he is in love with his mother and hates his father, that he is the unfortunate possessor of an oedipus complex, that he is an anal character or runs around as an oral personality, that he really feels castrated or that he is overwhelmed by an archetype. It is true that such information may shock my counselee out of the complacency of his everyday interpretation of his experience and behavior. My explanations may set him on the road of real presence to his experiences as they really are. The problem, however, is that these scientific explanations are not necessarily covering his true experience. It may very well be that my counselee unwittingly substitutes for the experience of daily life an artificial made-up scientific experience. Instead of exploring the intimate structure and meaning of experience itself, he simply accepts the scientific interpretation which I hand to him and continues his alienation from his true self in a more sophisticated way than before. Where he was first caught in a prison of naive interpretation, he is now trapped in a quasiscientific form of subjectivism, which might distort the given phenomenon even more than his previous naive explanation.

Counselor and counselee both may be the victim of this scientific subjectivism. They both may "perceive," for example, in the experience of the counselee inferiority feelings, projections, archetypes, repressions, reinforcements, resistances, castration and oedipus complexes, transference, rationalizations, sublimations, and the like. This artificial scientific experience is learned in the form of a language which provides the counselee with a ready systematic explanation of all his behavior in a way that satisfies his rationality and that therefore may lessen his anxiety without really bringing him into contact with his true self.

When we look somewhat closer at this artificial scientific *experience*, we realize that it is the abortive result of two sources. One source of scientific self-experience is the naive experience of everyday life; the other source is the immediate interpretation of this naive natural experience by means of the categories of established scientific theories. Such a scientific interpretation, especially when it is premature, prevents a respectful attention to the inner structure and meaning of experience in the unique life situation of the client. Consequently, established intersubjectivistic theoretical influences are substituted for or added to the subjectivistic distortions of everyday explanations which are already inserted in the naive experience itself. This impoverished, scientifically made-over experience is then considered as the full real experience, a substitute for the real underlying experience which the client is supposed to have. This scientific experience is called "fact," and this fact is then hailed by the counselor as the true original experience of the counselee which he was able to uncover for the first time by means of his scientific categories. The collection and enumeration of these facts enables the scientific counselor to arrive by induction at the establishment of laws which should rule the process of counseling. In this way, the counselor may develop a system of counseling autonomously, in a way closed in upon itself, an empty game with splendid categories irrelevant to real experience of people in vital situations, a mythology of behavior which claims to explain everything while it explains nothing.

Obviously I can do much harm as a counselor when

my perception of the client and his communication is distorted by the premature introduction of theoretical explanations. If I am a good counselor, I will penetrate first into behavior and experience as it manifests itself and only then ponder how existing theories of personality may illumine this experience without distortion. I should remain open for the possibility that such scientific theories should be corrected, expanded, or renewed to keep in touch with behavior as given in reality today and as faced by me in the counseling situation. Theories of personality and psychotherapy should supplement rather than supplant my understanding. To be sure, I may draw on the rich fund of past insight and experience called "theories of personality," but my prudent selection from this treasure-trove of theoretical explanations should be illumined by real behavior as it manifests itself in my client. My primary commitment is to existence, not to a theory about existence, even an existential theory. My openness for the communications of my counselee should enable me not only to spot the relevant theoretical explanation but also to adapt it to the concrete situation or even to improve it on the basis of my receptive observation. In the latter case, I may possibly enrich the treasure of psychology so that others after me may have more knowledge available about possible human experiences than I originally had.

It should be my wish, however, that my successors will neither abuse my descriptions or discoveries for the distortion of their data, or substitute my observation for their perception. It should be my hope that they may be more sensitive to behavior and experience than to my explanations about behavior and experience, that their ears may not be deafened by the noise of theories, and that their eyes may not be blinded by solemn expositions in journals, books, and papers, even if they happen to be my own.

Language Habit

In service of the same authentic openness for the real existence of my counselee, I should be aware of the fact that language habits or the daily or scientific use of language may interfere with my presence to experience as it really is. All kinds of psychological theories and categories may be embodied not only in scientific but also in prescientific language. English, for instance, is a prescientific language; the psychoanalytic, behavioristic, or introspectionistic idiom is a scientific language. I have to be constantly aware that language can never be the experience itself of my counselee but only a limited inadequate expression of this experience. Unfortunately, language is as apt to reveal as to conceal the experience which it tries to bring to expression. Often the words which my client uses may communicate much more than his experience. His words may express, for example, also the prescientific explanation of his experience, which he has received from his culture in the package of his language. In that case, our language habits convey not only the expression of experience but also the prescientific explanation of this experience. The population has created at a certain point in the history of our language this biased and selective expression which continues to distort true experience. Such an expression may conceal various aspects of the experience which fall outside the scope of the prescientific theory and which happen to dominate the mode of my civilization, and therewith the cast of our language.

Let me try to illustrate this possibility by comparing one expression of the English language with a similar expression in Dutch and German. We select for our example the term "experience." We choose this word not because it is so terribly important for psychotherapy but only in order to make our point clear that theory influences language. The Dutch word for experience is "believing" or "ervaring"; the German is "erlebnis" or "erfahrung." When we use in Dutch or German respectively "ervaring" and "erfahrung" we point to an awareness in the past, for example, in the sentence: He is a man of great experience. The Dutch "believing" and the German "erlebnis" however have a quite different meaning. Both words are derived from respectively the Dutch "beleven" and the German "erleben" which literally means "to live an event, to be in the lively presence of an event," for "beleven" and "erleben" connote respectively "leven" and "leben" which mean "to live." This expression denotes thus in both languages the actuality of a lively presence of the subject to a reality here and how. The term "experience" in the English language, however, has lost this meaning under the impact of a powerful British stream of thought called "empiricism."

As a result, the term "experience" in English always points to something that happened in the past, it never indicates my lively intuition of something in the present. English simply does not have a word for this experience because empiricism did not believe in this lively intuitive presence in the very present. Consequently, when I use this word experience to express a present experience, I may obscure or falsify my perception and the perception of my client. Both of us led by the language may overlook or misinterpret the behavior or experience which is an actual "lived" presence of the subject to reality without reflection. When I, however, momentarily suspend the language habit and put the meaning of conventional language as it were, in parentheses, I may rediscover this possibility of human experience, the awareness of which was lost in our language after its impoverishment under the influence of empiricism. The rediscovery of such a forgotten or concealed reality of human life may force me to enrich my language with a new expression which points to the forgotten phenomenon. I may speak, for instance, of "lived" experience, or "lived" awareness.

This is only an example to illustrate that I, as a counselor, should always be ready to transcend my language in faithfulness to experience and behavior. Language is the treasure-trove of accumulated theories, insights, and observations developed by a people in the current of its history; the fascinating history of a standing-out together in certain ways toward reality. This shared existence toward reality makes reality reveal itself in peculiar ways to the cultural coexistents. The resulting insights are conserved in the constituted language of a people. This constituted language should be a help, not a hindrance, toward further unconcealment of reality in my client; it should not suppress but support living language in the counseling hour, not fossilize but foster vision, not limit but expand perception in both counselor and counselee.

The same is true of constituted *scientific* language which presents a similar problem. Psychoanalytic, behavioristic, or organismic terminology should not paralyze but nurture the openness of the counselor, should not limit but expand his perception and vision. The counselor might profit fully from the treasure of scientific language if he is able to free himself temporarily from its influence on his perception. Perception unadulterated by theoretical tenets prepares him for a new appreciation of what other theorists have seen before him. If he then looks again at the position of the

theorists of personality, he will be aware of their inherent limitations because of his previous open perception of "behavior-as-it-is."

What we have described here amounts to a description of two attitudes which should accompany openness, namely, the attitude of suspension and vigilance,
suspension of all theories embedded in prescientific
and scientific language, and vigilance against the premature intrusion of such theories. Only when his
openness is safeguarded by these two attitudes will the
counselor be able to encounter his client beyond
theory and classification. Only afterwards may I see in
what sense and to what degree I may characterize
their behavior by constructs *about* behavior. Scientific
psychology becomes then a light that enlightens, not a
veil that dims the perception of the counselor.

CHAPTER VII

THE GOALS OF COUNSELING
AND PSYCHOTHERAPY FROM
THE EXISTENTIAL VIEWPOINT

THE traditional schools of psychology and psychiatry provide us with a great deal of information concerning factors which make it difficult for people to allow themselves free insight into their behavior and perception. The various psychoanalytic schools especially can help the counselor to become sensitive to the various impediments which make it difficult for his client to perceive in freedom his own existence. The learning theories of behaviorism give the counselor a wealth of scientific data concerning the conditioning of behavior in the counselee.

Existential psychology describes the human person in a balanced way. It acknowledges respectfully the contributions of psychologies which focus on the determined aspects of man's personality, but at the same time it insists on the free responsibility and spontaneous creativity which remain the unique and fundamental characteristics of human existence even when they are defective, slightly developed, or almost lost. Existential psychology retains awareness of the limits of freedom revealed by the psychologies of factual determinants, yet it transcends determinism by its recognition of man's radical freedom which is equally observable in his behavior as his physiological and environmental determinants. The existential psychology of man could be defined as a psychology of man as limited in freedom.

What is man like when he has been set free by psychotherapy? As a psychotherapist, I address myself to a fellow human being. I see and experience him as a person called to actualize himself within his unique life situation. He came to me because he felt vaguely that something was wrong; he was dissatisfied with his life, his existence seemed dreary, meaningless, and without value; he was in trouble with people around him, in his daily work, and within himself; he suffered from disturbing symptoms which diminished his efficiency. I can briefly summarize his feelings and symptoms by saying that my client had lost the ability to understand and to realize the unique meaning of his existence within his unique life situation. Therefore, as a good therapist, I must foster an atmosphere which will enable him to understand himself within his situation and to face his personal responsibility.

Openness to Authentic Guilt

My client must recognize and work through his own authentic guilt instead of becoming fixated on his neurotic guilt. During this process of growth I should be careful not to burden him with my personal feelings of guilt, with my own expectations, or with norms which dominate the cultural structures to which I personally have committed myself. Authentic guilt, responsibility, and commitment must grow out of his own true experiences. They must be truly his and not mine. He must find his own personal response to his reality independent of my response to my reality. He cannot become "whole" if he does not discover his own decisive answer to his own life but blindly incorporates my personal answers which may be alien to his very individuality. If he blindly adopts my personal style of existence, he will foster a harmful split between his own unclarified self and my superimposed self. My client can reach wholeness only if he discovers his own authentic guilt which is covered over by layers of neurotic guilt. He has a right to his own guilt; psychotherapy should enable him to discover this personal guilt which is linked with a personal experience of responsibility for his own becoming.

Dynamic Existence

Psychotherapy will enable my client not only to discover his true guilt and responsibility but also to experience that life is growth, development, and actualization. This growth may take the form of freeing himself from the paralyzing influence of a one-sided mode of existence, or it may mean the development of new authentic modes. Growth also implies the integration of old and new modes of existence into a wholesome style of life. The liberation from inauthentic modes is characteristic of the initial phase of psychotherapy. The discovery of hidden repressed modes of being and the development of new authentic ones are prevalent in the second period of therapy. The integration of newly emerged with past authentic modes of existence into a new style of life appears more clearly at the end of the therapeutic process. Of course, these three movements of growth are not mutually exclusive. On the contrary, they coincide. We can say only that one or the other is more dominant at a certain stage of the therapeutic process.

My client's therapeutic experience that his life is growth and becoming implies his acceptance of the fact that his personality will never be "finished" or "totally understood" or even "without mystery or problem," or that he will always be on the road, always a traveller, an adventurer, a pioneer who never reaches the far West of his full existence. The final aim of psychotherapy is, thus, full acceptance of a dynamic existence opening up to continually new horizons.

Such therapy will enable my client to adapt himself continually to his own emerging possibilities of being and to realize these possibilities in his life. For the human self reveals itself in constantly new aspects to be actualized. Neither therapist nor client can predict the appeals of tomorrow. But therapy can create a readiness to listen to the challenges which will announce themselves. I think, therefore, that it is crucial for my client to grow to the insight that his actual personality is not unchangeable.

When I say "actual personality," I mean the structural totality and specificity of the modes of existence which my client has developed up to this moment of crisis in his life. He may believe that his personality is fixed forever. He may perceive himself as a thing molded once and for all. He may use his belief in his unchangeability as an escape from the burden of becoming. Thereapy should enable my client to become aware of what is authentic and inauthentic in this view of himself. There are various authentic structures of personality which can emerge from the deepest core of his being when he is in dialogue with his various life situations; for every individual has deep within himself a unique potential structure of existence which can be realized in a variety of superstructures. This fundamental structure, or infrastructure, cannot be changed without violating him as an individual. What can change, however, is the concrete realization of this hidden structure.

My client came to me because of his failure to actualize this unique structure, which he fundamentally is. In other words, the constellation of his actual modes of existence is inauthentic because of his anxious introjection of foreign elements which are at odds with what he basically is. This situation makes it impossible for him to be what he should be in his concrete daily existence. This constellation of adopted actual modes of existence may cover up this unique style of being which is truly his. No therapy, to be sure, can give the client an exhaustive understanding of all that he is. Good therapy, however, will enable him to discover and realize himself increasingly in the infinite plurality of encounters in his daily life during, and especially after, the time that he is in therapy.

One of the bases of the unique style of each human existence is that each individual has his own typical constellation of those drives, impulses, and basic motives which are characteristic of our species. These fundamental forces are present in every human being at least potentially. But their relative strength and actual intensity, their mutual relationships and their fundamental configuration differ from individual to individual. I do not speak here about differences due to environment, education, and personal life situation, but about those more basic differences which are given from the outset as the raw material of human personalities. It is true that everyone of my clients will eventually decide on the fundamental orientation of his existence, his existential project in the light of his life situation. Yet, the specific style of his existence or the concrete embodiment of his project will emerge from his uniquely given constellation of forces which we call drives, inclinations, impulses, and motives. Openness to both his life situation and the unique power configuration of his dynamic forces will lead gradually to his authentic and unique style of existence. For this reason, theoretical simplification or reduction of the complexity of human existence by the therapist is potentially harmful. This does not mean that psychological theories are useless. On the contrary, each scientifically acceptable hypothesis enriches the therapist with a new possibility for understanding certain realms of experience in his clients. The existential attitude in psychotherapy, however, implies the use of these acquired sensitivities within a wide openness for the infinite variety of possibilities of human existence.

For example, my client's preoccupation with study *can* be an expression of sexual curiosity, a compensation for a feeling of inferiority, an escape from social life, sheer pleasure in the intellectual, dedication to a cause, or a form of obedience to parents, school, or other institutions. But this involvement in study may also be a result of an irreducible unique predisposition. In the latter case, it is a natural expression of the unique personality structure of my client and not a reactive phenomenon. Of course, many reactive motivations may be present together in my client. In this case, they may influence one another. But, this does not mean that I can a priori consider one motivation and its contributions to a subsequent mode of existence as merely a derivation of another motive which co-constitutes a certain mode of existence. For example, sexual curiosity may lead to a more generalized intellectual curiosity and influence its development. This does not mean that intellectual curiosity can be reduced to mere sexual curiosity.

Liberation from Psychologism, Public Image, Scientism

The person who comes for psychotherapy today is frequently influenced by certain reducing concepts of psychology and psychiatry which are popularized by the mass media of communication. He may not realize that each one of these various theories reveals only certain possible aspects of human existence and by no means all possible aspects. As a result he may begin to see himself almost solely in the light of one or the other psychological theory. Such a narrowed consideration of his personality will lead necessarily to a blindness for those possibilities of selfhood which are not emphasized by the particular theory in question. Many people are crippled in their personality development by the influence of popularized psychology and psychiatry. Therefore, one of the long-range aims of contemporary therapy is to liberate people from the tyranny of popular concepts, which, like a thick fog, render real personal self-experience impossible.

Another purpose of psychotherapy today is to enable the client to free himself from another tyranny, the despotism of the public image. Government and industry, schools and social organizations, the worlds of entertainment and even of religions are unhealthily conscious of how they appear in the eyes of others. The promotion of an attractive image is an ongoing concern, an anxious preoccupation. An individual who is deeply influenced by such concern ceases to be a real person. He cares more about how he looks to others than about what he is. He is more sensitive to the preferences of others than to his own feelings. He is inspired by the ideals of the majority rather than those ideals which are in harmony with his own deepest being. If the demon of the public image takes firm possession of him, he becomes unable to distinguish between his own feelings and the impersonal urges of the crowd. My client may have risen to the heights of administrative, academic, political, or ecclesiastical success by his clever catering to the crowd or to his superiors. He may not be consciously aware that he has paid the highest price for this popularity, his own priceless individuality. The more intelligent, creative, and idealistic the client is, the deeper he will be disturbed by his selling out, by the prostitution of his talents. His most profound self may be compared to a call girl available to the best paying patron and obligingly conforming to his every wish.

Preoccupation with the public image has become a cultural disease which has led many potentially creative individuals to an apathetic, improverished life of quiet desperation. Many such men, suffering from a meaningless existence, present themselves for therapy.

In this case, one of the aims of therapy is to help them to discover their own individuality under the mask of their public image.

I consider another aim of contemporary therapy to be the gradual growth of an attitude which I would call "patient self-presence." Many people come into therapy with the fantasy that they will enjoy flashes of insight which will lead to sudden changes in their lives. This expectancy of self-improvement as a result of therapeutic manipulation is due not only to "magic" thinking but also to the "scientistic" attitude fostered in our civilization. Physical science, the explorations and manipulations of physical objects, is desirable in its own realm. But scientism, or the expansion of the methods of physical science to nonphysical subjects such as human existence, the free project of life, and the growth of the self is most undesirable. It is not a clearly formulated doctrine but an all pervasive mode of being which is assumed, especially by those who know little about science itself. This attitude of scientism leads its victims to manipulate their lives as if they were physical objects, algebraic equations, or experiments in chemistry. Such people may come into therapy convinced that their main problem is that they have not yet found the efficient method or technique for successful self-manipulation. Their scientistic mode of existence leads them to expect a fast diagnosis and an effective "recipe" for a swift metamorphosis of their personality. One of the chief things they learn in psychotherapy is that one cannot deal with a false mode of existence as with a diseased leg or liver, that an attempted equation of psychological with physical healing is misleading.

In the long, sometimes tedious process of psychotherapy, these clients experience that an unwholesome mode of existence is usually formed by an accumulation of experiences over a long period of time. They realize gradually and slowly that the manifold experiences which built this unsavory mode of being were not worked through at the moment that they were introjected; they were not freely and wisely appropriated. The clients now see, in the process of therapy itself, that not only the insight into the complex structure of a mode of existence, but also the slow and painful growth beyond this mode, requires an arduous and patient dialogue with the myriad manifestations of this mode in innumerable concrete life situations. Therapy is the development of the ability for persevering dialogue with the disclosures of one's existence in daily life. One of the long-range aims of psychotherapy, therefore, is to prepare the client to be patiently present to himself as manifested in his life situation. This art often remains unlearned in our technological society.

Openness to Authentic Conflict

I do not believe that it is the aim of psychotherapy to solve all conflicts and problems of the client. Psychotherapy helps man to uncover the unique fundamental structure of his personality and to commit himself to the actualization of this structure. Therapy helps him to transcend the spurious and inauthentic structures which superseded his authentic being. It strengthens him against both the demon of the public image and his scientistic inclination to self-manipulation. He develops from a mechanic of life into a living person, but this does not mean that he will not be faced with contradictions and conflicts within his personality. Contradiction and conflict are potentially present in his basic given structure of existence. The various modes of being in the world which he can develop on the basis of his true self must be balanced and integrated with one another. The aim of psychotherapy is not to solve his conflicts but to enable him to see and experience these opposed inclinations more clearly within himself. Psychotherapy brings to light what the person is and sets him on the path of becoming what he is to be. It changes neither the unique and fundamental structure of his existence nor its inherent conflicts and contradictions. The end of therapy is the beginning of conflict. Once man has come to himself through psychotherapy he is able to discover, maintain, and restore the balance between the opposing forces which are characteristic of his unique personality. A client may discover, for example, an inclination to dependency which may not be reducible to any other "cause" in his past or in his environment but which is truly inherent in the very structure of his existence. In this case, he himself must take his stand toward this inclination and learn how to live wisely with this particular expression of himself in his life situation. In this sense, we may say that it is an aim of psychotherapy to initiate authentic conflict which replaces the inauthentic conflicts of the client's past.

Having reviewed these general aims, I may now become somewhat more specific in analyzing the main attitudes which I expect to develop in my client after successful therapy.

Existential Honesty

I consider it one of the long-range aims of psychotherapy that my client will be able to be true to himself and to others. One of the outcomes of therapy should be that the client is able to recognize his own identity, that he knows what he himself thinks and feels about the various aspects of his life situation. This does not mean, of course, that he takes into account only his own perceptions. It means that ultimately only he himself must make the final decisions in his life according to his own personal insight, which is enriched, deepened, and tempered by a personal evaluation of the insights of others. This basic honesty implies that my client has learned in psychotherapy to abdicate all attitudes, actions, customs, words, and expressions which he experiences as untrue. This striving to diminish in his existence the strength of the defensive systems which he has developed in anxious self-protection must continue after therapy. This task is never finished, for the defensive and neurotic systems of existence always remain available in the personality and reemerge immediately when the person feels threatened. So long as he does not develop this fundamental and courageous honesty, he will not be able to achieve an authentic human existence.

Why is it so difficult for my client to abdicate all that is not authentically human? I think that a deep existential anxiety makes my client hold on so desperately and tenaciously to his defensive attitudes. Deep down he is aware that up to now his real potential self-structure could not actualize itself, smothered as it was by the powerful defensive structures of his existence. He realizes, therefore, that the loss of his "borrowed feathers" would reveal him in the ugly nudity of a not yet actualized personality. On a deep level, this perception gives him the anxious feeling that he is entering an emptiness in which he will lose all his moorings and certitudes. Thus, his resistance to honesty is not so much a matter of bad will as of anxiety at seeing and revealing himself as small, weak, and insufficient.

Everyone wants to be somebody, a person who counts. Man is perhaps most afraid of the possible discovery that he is really unimportant. It would be easier, perhaps, for my client to accept himself as bad than as insignificant. Frequently, his inclination to attract the attention of others arises from a defense against his anxiety that he may discover his own insignificance rather than from a real belief in his own importance. My client may feel, unconsciously, so unimportant and meaningless that he is overwhelmed by the constant fear that others may see him in the same way if he surrenders his make-believe attitudes and behavior. His secret perception of himself as small and worthless opens up for him a world in which people are constantly on the verge of discovering him. It is understandable that this fear leads to a forced and spasmodic concentration on his own behavior, words, and expressions.

Therefore, when the client begins to give up his defensiveness, his behavior becomes immediately freer, more relaxed and natural, less tense and guarded. This breakdown of the old defensive structure is already, in and by itself, an expression of the new man. It is true that at first the client may appear less forceful and certain than before. However, the strength which he shows now, no matter how little, is truly the force of his own being and, therefore, far stronger than his artificial, self-conscious attitude of the past which may indeed have seemed very impressive to weak people in his environment. This new authentic strength, when he maintains it after therapy, will gain in depth; it will be free from the anxiety which invested so much energy in former defensive structures. Sooner or later this authentic strength, which the person really is, will influence others far more deeply than the former show of force or cleverness and the past pretense of power and unshakable self-reliance. At the moment that my client dares to be small, worthless, and unimportant, he is no longer the insignificant man which he was, because the very courage to be what he is endows him with the radiance of a significant, inalienable existence.

This basic honesty gained in psychotherapy also enables my client to admit his own mistakes easily and swiftly. In the past he was afraid that any mistakes he made would jeopardize his very existence or destroy the esteem which he had in the eyes of others. He was inclined to identify his whole personality with his duty in society. If anyone attacked his work or devaluated his contribution, he experienced it as an attack on his very personality. He felt threatened in the core of his existence. It is one of the long-range aims of psychotherapy to make it possible for the client in his future life to understand his mistakes as signposts of improvement and growth. He must be able to risk himself in the life situation. He must dare to make mistakes and to accept the consequences of these mistakes without anxiety, bitterness, and resentment. One direct result of this newly acquired attitude will be a gain in his creativity and productivity. For creativity and effective presence to the life situation are frequently blocked by anxiety about making mistakes. Creativity can flourish only when a person feels free to be found imperfect and prone to failure. Many people lead ineffective lives because they feel compelled to retire as soon as they make mistakes and are blamed for them.

Of course, it will take a lifetime to make concrete in daily endeavor this basic honesty which the client has found in psychotherapy. In the realization of his honest self-insight, he will time and time again discover resistances in himself. Therapy should establish a readiness to cope with these resistances, a willingness not to be more nor less than he really is, but to be faithful to the task which is imposed by his life situation.

Existential Commitment

The readiness to listen to the appeal of the life situation implies commitment. Existential commitment means that my client has given up his self-centered, autocratic existence and put himself at the disposal of the demands of life. This does not mean that he surrenders himself blindly to another person or institution, but that he is willing to live a project of life that, according to his own insight, is in tune with the realistic demands of existence. Instead of saying, "I decide what I like to do," he now says, "I personally decide what is asked of me in my life situation." What he gives up is not his own judgment, insight, freedom, and responsibility but his egocentrism. He refuses to make his egoistic concern the last and only criterion of his life project. Rather, he responds freely to the life situation in which he finds himself, and he does so in harmony with his own being. This implies that my client experiences that there is something higher than himself. In other words, there is a suprapersonal element in his surrender. This surrender liberates him from his egocentric prison and integrates him within reality, life, and history.

The commitment at which therapy aims does not find its source in a greater confidence in one's isolated self. On the contrary, authentic self-confidence is more the outcome than the source of existential commitment. Free and relaxed self-confidence is rooted in the experience of one's integration in life, in culture and society, in nature, in the world of suprapersonal values, in being and its mysterious ground. If my client is religious, he may experience self-confidence because of his rootedness in the mystery of the divine. Existential commitment diminishes existential anxiety. Authentic freedom is not based on belief in one's own strength, but on joyful surrender to life with all the risks which it implies.

The client who leaves therapy with this attitude is less clear and certain about the concrete details of his future, but he is filled with trust that life will suggest to him the right solutions at the right time if he lives in a relaxed openness for all the messages which life may give him. Before therapy, anxiety about the unknown and the untried severely hindered his self-realization. Now, however, he feels ready for whatever may happen to him. His faith in existence, his surrender to being convinces him that he will find light to take the next step at every winding of the road of his life. He no longer feels that it is necessary for him to see the whole road clearly before he feels free to move.

Existential commitment implies the acceptance of existence in all its aspects whether they give rise to joy or pain. After successful psychotherapy, my client will be able to bear the suffering which is unavoidable in life. Before therapy, his growth was impaired by his attempts to avoid painful experiences. Now, however, he dares to expose himself to the reality of life. Doing so, he actualizes his possibility for a fuller and deeper understanding of human existence. Many aspects of life are revealed only in suffering that is faced and worked through. My client will be increasingly able to accept without fatalism or apathy, resistance or resentment, escape or avoidance the suffering which life brings to him. In other words, suffering is still present, is still painful; yet it does not disturb his inner freedom.

This ability to face suffering paradoxically enables my client to enjoy freely the gifts of his life. When one is afraid of suffering, he cannot enjoy the blessings of life in and for themselves. He uses them frantically in order to escape the burden of existence. While attempting to forget the painful aspects of existence in a wild enjoyment of life's pleasures, he is continually haunted by anxiety about the burdensome aspect of life that may reveal itself again when enjoyment ceases. He who cannot suffer fully is also unable to enjoy fully. People who are haunted by anxiety about pain are hesitant when the possibility of deep and intense joy reveals itself at certain moments of their existence. They prefer ephemeral pleasures to existential joy which touches the very core of their being. They are afraid that such a joy may create a possibility for the overwhelming pain. Fundamentally, they are right. For example, the overwhelming joy of a deep and unique love always implies the risk of overwhelming pain in case the beloved dies, disappears, or betrays one. Happiness entails a threat which may evoke anxiety.

Therefore, many clients are not able to enjoy with a full and relaxed presence the great gifts of life which have come their way. One manifestation of their anxiety is a lack of inner freedom in regard to what has been given to them. Their attitude is characterized by an anxious, possessive holding on to these gifts. This fearful preoccupation makes it impossible for them to enjoy really and fully; for authentic enjoyment is possible only if one accepts without afterthought the good gifts of life and is ready to let them go when they fade away. In other words, existential commitment is just as necessary for true enjoyment as for true suffering. Both are possible only if one surrenders in freedom to the mystery of existence. I do not mean that after psychotherapy my client should throw himself into joy or pain in blind surrender. Good therapy establishes a quiet openness for all aspects of life, which does not mean that the person lets himself be passively overwhelmed by happiness or suffering. Life is a gift and a task. Everyone has to decide in his concrete life situation how far a joy or a pain is a gift or a demand for action. The realistic openness acquired in psychotherapy will enable the client to determine to what degree they invite him to action.

Before psychotherapy, the client is inclined to avoid the appeal of the present by living in the past or the future. But he discovers in therapy that surrender to the mystery of existence always means a full presence to the situation here and now. He learns to accept every existential moment with all the risks and possibilities which it implies. For he has realized in the long process of psychotherapy that real life can only be lived today, not yesterday or tomorrow.

Thus, it is the aim of psychotherapy to prepare the client for a gradual transcendence of his self-centeredness in commitment to reality. He should experience that commitment to life, to his duty, to the demands of the present, to others is the necessary condition for an enhanced, unique personality. The real self grows only in self-commitment and realizes itself only in a transcendence of the inauthentic, defensive, or anxious self. This commitment is an expression of man's total readiness to make himself available to life as honestly understood in the light of his own unique possibilities. This free and total commitment leads to unity and integration in the personality of my client. He becomes one with himself. This unity leads to a new force and strength in his personality and in the execution of his daily assignments.

For example, a client who was a college teacher experienced great difficulties in the preparation of his lectures and in the composition of scholarly papers for presentation at conventions. One of the reasons why he experienced inner resistance and division during the performance of his duties was the fact that he was not wholly and freely committed to his study. He prepared his lectures and wrote his articles because he was concerned about the esteem of his students, colleagues, and superiors. He was not motivated by a real inner commitment to his writing and his teaching. As a result, his preparation was a chore that increasingly burdened and bored him. It became almost impossible for him to concentrate on the literature which he had to analyze in preparation for his classes. Just as soon as he sat down behind his desk with a stack of books and articles before him, he felt tired, exhausted, and disgusted. His mind wandered off in all directions, except that of his study.

What exhausted him was not the task itself but an inner conflict between what he himself desired to do and the demands imposed on him by his position as a teacher. He wanted and did not want to study. In fact, a considerable amount of his energy was invested in the struggle against his inner resistance to the task at hand. After therapy, however, he was a renewed man who was able to prepare his lectures effectively without the overwhelming fatigue which he formerly experienced. He had learned in therapy to commit himself to his task freely, to give up his inner resistance, and to conquer the split in his existence. All his energy was now available for the task at hand. This does not imply that his work no longer had unpleasant aspects, or that it lost its own intrinsic difficulties and problems. But the client's existential commitment made it possible for him to accept his task fully with all its pleasant and unpleasant angles. He became a relaxed, energetic, and well-prepared teacher.

Existential commitment determines whether or not a person will freely actualize his existence or will be stunted in his growth by inhibition, fixation, or perversion. Of course, such a commitment is not an act which is performed once and for all. After psychotherapy, my client must renew his commitment many times during his life. He must continually regain the

attitude of commitment and inner freedom; for his defensive, egocentric, and infantile structures never dis-
appear totally. Consequently, good therapy cannot
aim at once-and-for-all commitment. It aims at an attitude of self-commitment and a readiness to restore
free commitment every time that it is lost through external pressures and inner anxiety which lead to the
reemergence of defensive structures.

It is difficult for many clients to understand that
commitment leads to authentic self-confidence. Many
clients are successful businessmen, scholars, scientists,
or leaders who have achieved powerful political or ecclesiastical positions. They come into therapy because
of neurotic symptoms which make them uneasy and
less efficient than they would like to be. The idea of
commitment and surrender does not appeal to them.
Their outlook is precisely opposed to commitment.
They feel that they were able to gain power by looking
out for themselves, by clever manipulation of their environment, by the art of forming friendships and relationships which fostered their rise in society. They declare that people in their environment admire them for
their ruthless strength and harsh self-confidence. They
do not realize that concentration on their own success
has isolated them from the fullness of existence, that
manipulation of life and preoccupation with power,
possessions, and status lead to existential impoverishment and emptiness, and that such material success is

accompanied by loss of rich humanity. This is also true of those clients who demand love, friendship, and protection from others instead of giving to others. They do not understand that every time they demand something from life they isolate themselves from life. Man should learn not to ask what he can demand from life, but what life demands from him.

Sometimes during therapy a client may even be inclined to use commitment as a means of manipulation of his life. In this case he has not yet achieved authentic commitment because the latter, while being in tune with the uniqueness of the self, is not directed toward the self or its actualization as an ultimate aim. The person who attempts inauthentic commitment is still self-directed. All that happens to him is the expansion of his self-prison and the addition of a new weapon to his arsenal of manipulating devices. Only a commitment which is not self-centered but conscious and free has a liberating effect on human existence. Only such commitments makes man a full participant in the mystery of being and offers him a center from which he can live an integral life, undivided by egocentric tendencies.

The Acceptance of Oneself

Commitment to reality implies that my client accepts himself with respect. He assumes a responsibility for the gift which he himself is. He must realize his own unique potentialities and defend himself when necessary. Commitment to existence sometimes means that the client must learn to place himself in the foreground when he would prefer to retire because of anxiety, defensive modesty, or egocentric false humility. He must accept himself with both his gifts and his limitations as a life assignment. Some clients do injustice to their own existence by dedicating themselves to others to such a degree that they neglect to care for themselves. As a result, healthy and wholesome care for their own existence is often replaced by hidden pity and by complaint about themselves. Instead of boldly seeking their rights, they express unconscious dissatisfaction in small idiosyncrasies and in stubborn insistence on insignificant privileges.

Commitment to himself implies my client's will to become independent in his inner life. Too strong an attachment to his parents and his milieu will render it very difficult for him to commit himself to his own independent growth. Moreover, if my client did not receive from his parents the care and guidance which he needed for his development, he feels a deep lack in his personality. He seeks restlessly for the fulfillment of need which was not offered by his parents. As a result he becomes fixated on the search for parental love, tenderness, and protection. It is true that the psychotherapist can to some degree fulfill this need. Nevertheless, he can never really make up for all that the client missed in his childhood. The client must realize that something was really missing in his early life, a painful lack that cannot be completely filled at this later stage of his existence. Commitment here and now to reality means that he must be ready to accept consciously and freely the painful reality of his past, to assume responsibility for himself, and to renounce his unconscious search for fulfillment of infantile wishes which should have been satisfied when he was a child, but which unfortunately cannot be fulfilled now that he is an adult. Only when he is able to commit himself unconditionally to life, even at the cost of his personal fulfillment, will he be able to grow and to overcome this handicap. Only when the client consciously gives up his need for wish fulfillment can he discover in himself the existential value which he expected to receive from outside himself.

The deed of commitment helps the client to develop modes of existence which were unjustly withheld from him as a child. This does not mean that he will not need others for his full development. It means, however, that he cannot expect others to orient themselves toward him spontaneously as if he were a young child. He must realize that he will receive the love and the dedication of others only by going out toward others. The more he goes out toward others, the more he will receive the love that he missed so much as a child. Of course it is initially impossible for the client to understand this possibility of receiving love for love. The therapist, therefore, must ease the way by showing un-conditional care and interest in the client. On the other hand, he does not treat the client as a mother treats her baby, for this would confirm the client in his infantile needs. Successful therapy, however, will pre-pare the client for commitment to life and others in spite of infantile needs. This commitment in turn will help the person to experience increasingly the love of others whom he will meet in his many encounters dur-ing and after psychotherapy.

Sometimes a client cannot reach independence and full commitment to his own life because of a con-stantly negative relationship to his parents and to other figures who later replace his parents. In this case, the person tries to free himself by attacking the ideas, feelings, and the life style of parents and parent fig-ures. He complains about their old-fashioned ideas; he tries to subject and to conquer them so that they will think, feel, and act in the same way as he himself does. This attempt leads to a new kind of dependency in the client; that is, his need to direct the thought and the life style of others and to force them to agree with him renders him most dependent upon them in his inner life. He is continually distressed by the different way in which older people or superiors live and act. His emo-tional life is very much bound by this negativity, which makes him unhappy, tense, and frustrated. Therapy aims at the liberation of the person from these nega-tive, as well as positive, bindings. Only after this liberation can the client freely grow in his relationship to parents and to parent figures whom he meets in the course of his life.

In this chapter I have discussed some of the long-range aims of psychotherapy. I have considered it the ultimate purpose of psychotherapy to awaken those possibilities for openness and growth which emerge from a true therapeutic liberation. Psychotherapy is a process in which a person is set free so that he may actualize his unique self in his unique life situation in accordance with the demands of reality. I described the many attitudes and characteristics which are typical of a person set free by psychotherapy and living the fuller life at which psychotherapy aims. Ideally, this person has gained an openness to his true and personal guilt which helps him to become aware of the moments in which he is unfaithful to his real self. Instead of a static life, he lives a dynamic existence opening up to continually new horizons, which implies his readiness to adapt himself continually to his newly emerging possibilities of being. He is open and faithful to his own fundamental potential structure of existence while remaining flexible in regard to the concrete structures in which this potential structure may express itself. He constantly purifies his self-awareness from the distorting influence of reductionistic psychologism, of the tyranny of the public image, and of scientism. He courageously accepts and faces the challenges of authentic inner conflict. He develops the attitude of existential honesty, which implies both an awareness of his defensive inauthentic structures and a readiness to weaken their impact on his daily life. This existential honesty also makes him willing to admit his limitations and mistakes and to accept, without panic, their consequences.

Psychotherapy, moreover, aims at the development of existential commitment in the client. Commitment implies his willingness to live a project of life which, according to his own insight, is in tune with the demands of reality. He now places the source of his self-confidence not in himself but in reality and its ground. Existential commitment also means the full acceptance of both the joyful and the painful aspects of reality. This commitment, moreover, leads to an undivided presence to the task of here and now. Finally, therapy aims at the client's acceptance of himself, which implies self-respect and a healthy standing up for his own rights. This respectful self-acceptance also means his willingness to grow in inner independence from parents, parent figures, and his environment.

These are the attitudes and characteristics which I see as some of the long-range aims of both counseling and psychotherapy. I realize, of course, that these are ideal aims which will probably never be realized totally in a client. Many clients are living under such handicaps that we cannot hope for their total liberation and the resulting fullness of existence at which therapy ultimately aims. The ideal aims of psychotherapy are a guide, an orientation, a beacon pointing the way. They tell us what we should strive for, even if a client can realize the ideal only to a modest degree.

SELECTED BIBLIOGRAPHY

Allport, Gordon W. The Psychology of Participation. *Psychological Review*. 53, 1945, 117-132.

Becoming. New Haven: Yale University, 1955.

Personality and Social Encounter. Boston: Beacon Press, 1960.

Pattern and Growth in Personality. New York: Holt, Rinehart and Winston, 1961.

Buytendijk, F.J.J. *La Femme*. Burges: Editions Desclee de Brouwer, 1954.

Phenomenologie de la rencontre. Paris: Desclee de Brouwer, 1952.

De Vrouw. Haar Verschinjning, Natuur en Bestaan. Utrecht, Holland: Spectrum, 1951.

Curran, Charles A. *Counseling in Catholic Life and Education*. New York: Macmillan, 1952.

Personality Factors in Counseling. New York: Grune and Stratton, 1945.

Gurwitsch, A. *Field of Consciousness*. Pittsburgh: Duquesne University Press, 1960.

The Phenomenological and the Psychological Approach to Consciousness. *Phil. Phenomenol. Res.* 15, 1954-55, 303-319.

Heidegger, Martin. *Existence and Being*. Introduction by Werner Brock. Chicago: Henry Regnery Company, 1949.

Essays in Metaphysics, trans. Kurt F. Leidecker. New York: Wisdom Library, a division of Philosophical Library, Inc., 1960.

An Introduction to Metaphysics, trans. Ralph Manheim. New Haven: Yale University Press, 1959.

The Question of Being, trans. William Kluback and Jean Wilde. New York: Twayne Publishers, Inc., 1958.

Being and Time. New York: Harper Bros., 1962.

Kwant, Remy. *From Phenomenology to Metaphysics*. Pittsburgh: Duquesne University Press, 1966.

The Phenomenological Philosophy of Merleau-Ponty. Pittsburgh: Duquesne University Press, 1963.

Phenomenology of Language. Pittsburgh: Duquesne University Press, 1965.

Encounter. Pittsburgh: Duquesne University Press, 1960.

Luijpen, William A. *Phenomenology and Atheism*. Pittsburgh: Duquesne University Press, 1966.

Existential Phenomenology. Pittsburgh: Duquesne University Press, 1960.

Phenomenology and Metaphysics. Pittsburgh: Duquesne University Press, 1965.

De Psychologie Van De Verveling. Amsterdam: H.J. Paris, 1951.

Marcel, Gabriel. *Man Against Mass Society,* trans. G.S. Fraser. Chicago: Henry Regnery Company, 1950.

The Mystery of Being. 2 Vols. Trans. Rene Hague. Chicago: Henry Regnery Company, 1950.

Being and Having. London: Dacre Press, 1949.

Maslow, Abraham H. A Theory of Motivation. *Psychological Review*. 50, 1943, 370-396.

Resistance to Acculturation. *Journal Soc. Issues,* 7, 1951, 26-29.

Motivation and Personality. New York: Harper Bros., 1959.

New Knowledge in Human Values. New York: Harper Bros., 1959.

Maslow, Abraham, H. and Mittelmann, B. *Principles of Abnormal Psychology*. New York, Harper Bros., 1941.

May, Rollo, (ed) *Existential Psychology*. New York: Random House, 1961.

Toward the Ontological Basis of Psychotherapy. *Existential Inquiries*. I, September, 1959, 5-7.

May, Rollo, Ernest Angel, and Henri F. Ellenberger. *Existence —A New Dimension in Psychiatry and Psychology*. New York: Basic Books, Inc., 1958.

Moustakeas, C. *Loneliness*. Englewood Cliffs, New Jersey: Prentice-Hall, Inc., 1961.

    The Teacher and the Child. New York: McGraw-Hill, 1956.

    The Self. New York: Harper Bros., 1956.

Rogers, Carl R. The Loneliness of Contemporary Man. *Review of Existential Psychology and Psychiatry*. I, Spring, 1961, 94-101.

    Counseling and Psychotherapy. New York: Houghton-Mifflin Co., 1942.

    Psychotherapy and Personality Change. Chicago: University of Chicago Press, 1954.

    On Becoming a Person. New York: Houghton Mifflin, 1961.

Rogers, Carl R. and Rosalind F. Dymond, eds., *Psychotherapy and Personality Change*. Chicago: University of Chicago Press, 1954.

Rogers, Carl R. and B. F. Skinner. Some Issues Concerning the Control of Human Behavior, *Science*, 124, 1956, 1057-1066.

Strasser, S. *The Soul in Metaphysical and Empirical Psychology*, trans. Henry J. Koren. Pittsburgh: Duquesne University Press, 1957.

    Phenomenology and the Human Sciences. Pittsburgh: Duquesne University Press, 1964.

van den Berg, J.H. and Buytendijk, F.J.J. (ed.) *Scientific Contributions to Phenomenological Psychology and Psychopathology*. Springfield, Illinois: Charles C. Thomas, 1955.

van den Berg, J.H. and Linschoten, J. *The Phenomenological Approach to Psychiatry. An Introduction to Recent Phenomenological Psychopathology*. Springfield, Illinois: Charles C. Thomas, 1955.

    Persoon en Wereld. Utrecht: Erven J. Bijleveld, 1953.

van Kaam, Adrian. Motivation and Contemporary Anxiety. *Humanitas* I, Spring, 1965, 59-76.

    A Light to the Gentiles. Milwaukee: Bruce Publishing Co., 1962.

    The Impact of Existential Phenomenology on the Psychological Literature of Western Europe. *Review of Existential Psychology and Psychiatry*. I, Winter, 1961, 63-92.

    Humanistic Psychology and Culture. *Journal of Humanistic*

Psychology. I, Spring, 1961, 94-100.

The Goals of Psychotherapy From the Existential Point of View. *The Goals of Psychotherapy,* ed. Alvin R. Mahrer. New York: Appleton-Century-Crofts, 1966.

The Fantasy of Romantic Love. *Modern Myths and Popular Fancies.* Pittsburgh: Duquesne University Press, 1961.

Existential and Humanistic Psychology. *Review of Existential Psychology and Psychiatry,* V, Fall, 1965, 291-297.

Existential Psychology. *The New Catholic Encyclopedia.* Washington, D.C.: The Catholic University of America, 1966.

The Existential Approach to Human Potentialities. *Explorations in Human Potentialities,* ed. Herbert A. Otto. Springfield, Illinois: Charles C. Thomas, 1966.

Counseling and Existential Psychology. *Harvard Educational Review.* Fall, 1962. This article was later published in *Guidance—An Examination,* New York: Harcourt, Brace & World, 1965.

Assumptions in Psychology. *Journal of Individual Psychology.* 14, 1958, 22-28.

The Addictive Personality. *Humanitas,* I, Fall, 1965, 183-194.

Personality Fulfillment in the Spiritual Life. Wilkes-Barre, Pa.: Dimension Books, Inc., 1966.

Religion and Existential Will. *Insight.* I, Summer, 1962.

Phenomenal Analysis: Exemplified by a Study of the Experience of 'Really Feeling Understood' *Journal of Individual Psychology.* 15, 1959, 66-72.

Religious Counseling of Seminarians. *Seminary Education in a Time of Change,* eds. James Michael Lee and Louis J. Putz. Notre Dame, Indiana: Fides Publishers, Inc., 1965.

Review of the Divided Self by R. D. Laing. *Review of Existential Psychology and Psychiatry.* II, Winter, 1962, 85-88.

Structures and Systems of Personality. *The New Catholic Encyclopedia.* Washington, D.C.: The Catholic University of America, 1966.

The Third Force in European Psychology. Greenville, Delaware: Psychosynthesis Research Foundation, 1960. (Greek translation, Athens, Greece, 1962.)

The Vocational Director and Counseling. Derby, New York: St. Paul Publications, 1962.

Existential Foundations of Psychology. Pittsburgh: Duquesne University Press, 1966.

INDEX

INDEX